STARS IN OUR EYES

STARS IN OUR EYES

Lee Darby

To order additional copies of this book, contact:
Xlibris
844-714-8691
www.Xlibris.com
Orders@Xlibris.com
826768

This book is dedicated to Anne and Rob. You were there, too. And to Liz and Brendan, of course.

My scrapbook opens to a photo of me naked in my crib in Corpus Christi, Texas, where my parents met while my father was stationed at the Naval Air Training Center during World War II. My birth announcement, bordered in pink, is from Lieutenant and Mrs. Joseph James Voye. Here is where my story unspools, as I celebrate the joy of writing it, the full dizzy eagerness of filling these pages with the output of my brain, of a past world noisy in my head, a past that has evolved for seventy plus years, curled tight as a tapeworm. When it uncoils, I hope it all makes sense to you for it is all true—the joys and the heartbreaks and tragedies, the shocking murder of my sister, and the beginning of the end of my life on earth.

★ ★ ★

We begin in the 1940s. My father's college education at Stanford was interrupted by the declaration of war after the attack on Pearl Harbor in December of 1941, and he joined the Marines. He trained to become a pilot in Pensacola, Florida, but instead of being sent overseas, he was selected to become a flight instructor. He said going into the air (as a pilot trainer of Corsair aircraft) with an eighteen-year-old rookie recruit was just as dangerous as a combat mission. His last posting was in Corpus Christi, Texas, where he met my mother, Patty, and they married in 1943. A picture in the scrapbook shows the two of them shin deep in Gulf surf, young, slim, and beautiful. Dad is holding a bottle of beer.

When Dad finished his military duty in Texas in 1946, he brought his bride, Patty, and infant daughter, Lee (me), to his hometown of Klamath Falls, Oregon, to stay with his parents while he decided what he wanted to do with his life after the military. Their second daughter, Sally, was born in 1947, and that year, Dad's father died at age fifty-eight. Dad said, as a kid, he hated having frozen hair in winter, which is one reason he transferred to Stanford University in 1940 after starting college at MIT in Boston. He had loved the area around Stanford, and in 1948, he decided to leave Klamath Falls and move to Menlo Park, where he had an uncle in business, to make a home there and raise his family.

At first, Dad worked in his uncle Bill's grocery store on Santa Cruz Avenue in Menlo Park but realized the life of a grocer was not for him. He loved math and numbers and, later, computers. He aimed to be an accountant and was studying for his certified public accounting degree.

Home was a white clapboard house on Ashton Street in Menlo Park, bought for $9,000 in 1948. Dad paid cash with help from his mother (his family didn't believe in mortgages); she also bought him a big black Buick. Our house had two bedrooms, a living room with a nubby green couch, polished wood floors, a kitchen with yellow linoleum and a drippy faucet, and one bath. Sally and I shared a bedroom. The backyard held a kiddie pool that Dad would blow up whenever the weather permitted, and Sally and I would splash around in it as the photos show, wearing our white cotton underpants. A chain-link fence surrounded the yard like a prison;

the fence was necessary because we had an Irish Setter, Danny Boy, who tried to break out every chance he could get. More than once when Mom and Dad were at a Stanford football game, there romped Danny Boy onto the football field, stopping the play, and Dad would have to go down to the field and take the dog home. Danny Boy eventually found a new home at a ranch out in the San Joaquin Valley, or so Dad said. There is a photo of Mom and Danny Boy with Sally and I wearing tartan plaid skirts that Mom made.

Next door was the Conner family in a big red two-story house. Mr. Conner was an ice man, delivering ice to businesses in a large square truck. Sally and I played with the boy named Stephen who lived across the street. His dad owned a coffee shop downtown on Santa Cruz Avenue. When I was five, I went to kindergarten at Las Lomitas School a few blocks away on Alameda de las Pulgas.

On my sixth birthday, the low October sun slanted across the dry leaves and gravel on the street in front of our little house. I rode my new blue bike around in circles as the light dimmed. I clenched the black rubber grips and turned my handlebars back and forth, searching and searching. Dust hung like glitter in the air, shining like the bright chrome on my new bike and the lights in our living room that I could see through the window. I could hear my father roar his great laugh at something my great-aunt or grandmother, who was visiting for my birthday celebration, must have said. His laugh usually set me to laughing, but instead, I was near tears. My fancy new ring, a birthday present from my grandmother, had somehow fallen off my finger as I rode my bike.

Gma was my father's mother. She dubbed herself "G (for grand)-ma," which worked out perfectly; my mother's mother had already staked a claim to the name Grandmother. Gma had given me the ring hours earlier, nestled in a black velvet box that opened with a creak, displaying a pink gemstone set in a circle of gold. It's a rose zircon, she said, as her sister, my great-aunt Agnes, nodded her head and warned me not to crack my knuckles or the joints would swell and I'd have problems with rings in my later years. I put the ring on and held out my arm to admire the way it captured the light. I'd never had a ring before, and it felt clumsy on my finger, like a Band-Aid, but it did make me feel more grown up. The black box, which I secretly admired just as much as the ring, went into my pocket, and I went outside to ride my new bike.

By the time I was called in to dinner, the dread had grown in my stomach and tightened my chest. My eyes ached with squinting at the graying pavement. I knew I must soon go in. We would have our dinner, my baby brother would entertain from his playpen, and I would blow out the candles on my birthday cake with Sally's help. After dinner, my Gma would play the piano, and she and my great-aunt would sing old hymns, their high voices trembling, and my father would have tears in his eyes. Later, they would play cards, and my father would win at Hearts every time, and he'd laugh and gloat. The crickets began to sound as I walked my bike slowly up to the porch steps and propped it on its kickstand. The moon was already showing luminous, the lunar pull of tide as strong as my dread of facing the giants, confessing my failure, my irresponsibility. A last shaft of sunlight poured through a break in the clouds, silhouetting the wired towers of the PG&E substation at the end of our street. I had one last hope of finding the ring and holding it to the light, precious, its facets catching the cold rays that were already beginning to glint in the evening sky. But no, Mom called me again to come in, my towheaded sister Sally looking on, curious. The ring was gone; it had dropped away into the soundless deep void where all lost things go. I opened the door, knowing how their fond smiles would dissolve when I told them.

By 1951, my parents had bought a lot in another neighborhood of Menlo Park (a cul-de-sac called Cotton Place). With the birth of my brother Rob, we had outgrown the little house on Ashton Street, and another baby was on the way. In our new neighborhood of ranch-style homes, many of the nearby streets were named after agricultural products, Cotton, Lemon, Olive, Bay Laurel, etc. My mother employed her college drafting skills to design a house in the modern style of Eichler, a popular design on the Peninsula at that time. My father, who by then had finished his accounting degree and gone to work as the financial controller for a heavy construction firm, inveigled various tradesmen and equipment operators to do a little extra work on weekends to help the project along. Mom and Dad subcontracted out the plumbing and electrical but did the painting and finishing and landscaping work even after we moved in in 1952. It seemed Mom was always dressed in painter's pants and splattered tennis shoes, her hair caught up in a bandana. The house was brick with redwood beams and shiny linoleum floors over a cement slab. All along the front sidewalk, grew a hedge of Meyer lemons that kept the bees busy most of the year. The branches' sharp thorns stuck us when we wanted to pick a few for lemonade. Sally and I loved roller skating on our skates that were clamped onto our tennis shoes with a metal key. We raced down the long hall lined with four bedrooms and two baths, but carpet installation in the hallway finally put the kibosh on that. Radiant heating coursed through pipes in the slab and made warm spots in the floor. The spot under the piano was my favorite, where I could curl up like a cat while Sally practiced the piano. The dining table was a hollow core door on sawhorses. Mom was proud of her modern kitchen with a disposal, a dishwasher, two ovens, and a refrigerator that spewed ice cubes from an opening in the door, right into Dad's cocktail glass and sometimes onto the floor (Dad muttered something we couldn't hear when that happened).

A wide covered patio, under which a ping-pong table and picnic table were located, looked out to a big square green lawn and garden. A ribbon of cement encircled the lawn so tricycles, bikes, and skates could zoom around smoothly. In the side yard, there was a swing set with tanbark for my brother Rob and our baby sister, Anne, to play on. Dad planted vegetables, and Mom planted some shrubs, including castor beans, which she liked because they were fast growers. She warned us that castor beans were poisonous and we shouldn't eat them.

Sally and I again shared a room with twin beds and a vinyl divider that pulled out like an accordion when we needed privacy or were feuding, but for the most part, we kept that divider pushed back against the wall, open. The flooring was linoleum squares with a white background and multicolor paint spatters like a Jackson Pollock canvas, very easy to clean according to Mom. We had matching quilts made by a friend of Gma's, and each of us had a stuffed bear. Mine was called Sugar; he was black and white. Her bear, brown and white, was called Spice. Sally and I made friends in the neighborhood, Lynn next door, Annette across the street, and Denise around the corner. Boys lived nearby, even Doug right next door, but I never got to know him well because he was a grade younger *and* playing with a boy was unthinkable for me. He was in Sally's grade, and she and Lynn spent time at his house, but he might as well have been a stranger to me. Similarly, the gulf of just a few years between me and Annette's older sister and Lynn's older brother prevented me from knowing them well either. Our cul-de-sac was a safe place to play baseball, kickball, or skate or play with your dog or just stroll over to pay someone a visit. Almost every house nearby had kids near our own ages. When we got old enough, we rode our bikes to Oak Knoll School about a mile away. I babysat for some of the neighbors once I was in seventh grade. Mom was the Parent-Teacher Association president several years running, and I would sometimes see her peek in the open doorway to my classroom and hear her high heels echo down the hallway to meet with the principal.

In my album is a picture of Sally and I in our dance recital costumes. We are holding hands like little elves. We took dance class downtown with Mrs. Crowder. Mom had to make the costumes out of rather stiff glittery fabric, including little hats like yarmulkes. Mom complained that every couple of stitches, she had to wipe the sticky glitter off the sewing machine needle.

★ ★ ★

When I was nine, Dad's employer transferred him and his family to Carpinteria, on the coast near Santa Barbara. The project he was assigned to was a highway under construction that would be completed in a year, so our house in Menlo Park was rented out, and we moved into a small rented house in Carpinteria on Calle Arena (Sand Street) that was right across the railroad tracks, and beyond that, thrillingly, was the Pacific Ocean, though you couldn't see it from the house because of the sand dunes. I have a photo of my brother, who was four, looking out the window and waving (he was supposed to be napping) as I came home from school. The nap was for Mom, of course.

All six of us would go down to the beach often to dig for clams, and we caught small fish called grunion in buckets, our footsteps fluorescing in the wet sand as the sun went down. Globs of tar dotted the beach from offshore oil wells. Mom used carbon tetrachloride to clean it off our feet when we got home. There always seemed to be sand in our beds and in our hair. The train would chug past daily, and we counted boxcars and flatcars by the dozen before the caboose came along and the guy in the caboose (what do you call the guy who is the opposite of the engineer in front?) always waved. I remember there were two boys who roamed about in our neighborhood, ones I observed but kept my distance. One was named Danny, and the other was named Tuffy. Once I heard Tuffy say, "Shet," which was the first four-letter word I had heard, not that I knew yet what it meant. Tuffy also sang, "Eeny, meeny, miny moe, catch a nigger by the toe . . ." Sally was indignant. She told him, "That's not nice!" She said that we always said "catch a tiger . . ." She didn't hesitate to say something when she observed unfairness. She had such a sense of justice, even in third grade.

I made a friend in my class named Cathie, who lived in the Rincon area. Our teacher in fourth grade at Aliso School was Mr. Hargis. After our year was up and we moved back to Menlo Park, I went on the train to stay with Cathie in Solana Beach where her family had moved. We went to the San Diego Zoo and the beach. Cathie was lovely and blonde and really smart; she ended up at Stanford. My scrapbook has a photo of her, in her high school blazer, looking proud and confident. I'm just now realizing that she was so much like Sally. Anyway, Cathie and I corresponded for years, but somehow, we lost touch in our twenties.

I'm sorry I lost her . . .

★★★

The best part of our summers was camp at Shady Lawn Farm. Grandmother wanted to send Sally and me to camp, and she selected Shady Lawn because somehow she found out the owners of the camp, Uncle Joe and Mother Roberts, were Christian Scientists. Grandmother was a lifelong devotee of Christian Science, hauling the four of us to church on Sundays. Sally and I went to Shady Lawn Farm for two weeks, and after the first year, we saved our allowances to pay for another week beyond what Grandmother could pay for. Our neighborhood friends Lynn and Denise listened to us rave about camp, and they started going too. Some of my most vivid memories are from those weeks each year.

Shady Lawn was located in Oakdale in the hot and dusty San Joaquin Valley. We rode horses every day, swam in the cold pool, sang camp songs, and made new friends. We sang "God Is Great and God Is Good, and We Thank Him for This Food" before meals in the big dining hall. There was red punch called Bug Juice, milk, and white bread and margarine on the tables, and though there were different main dishes like spaghetti, chicken, or burgers, there was always a tray of corn on the cob, grown right there on the farm. Every day I went through the buffet line with corn on my plate. Campers slept in bunk beds in what were various outbuildings serving the farm during the rest of the year. These quarters had names: Little House, Grape Arbor, Long Barn, and Cricket Lodge. The cement-block bathrooms were a short walk from the bunkhouses. There were showers, but who needed a shower when you swam every day? The counselors told us when it was our bunkhouse's turn to set up the tables for lunch or dinner. Craft House was where we experimented with lapidary, wood burning, leather stamping, beading, and lanyards woven with colorful plastic-covered flat string. Mom, Dad, and Grandmother got new key ring lanyards every year, whether they needed a new one or not. There was a rock polisher that made a terrible racket. I polished some pink stones and glued them to clips: earrings for Grandmother.

After lunch, we gathered on long benches at the outdoor meeting area to hear announcements and sing camp songs ("Fried ham, fried ham, cheese, and baloney . . ." or "Oh, give me a home, where the buffalo roam . . .") After that, we went to our bunkhouses and rested during the hottest part of the day. Mid-week, we got our camp T-shirts and had our bunkhouse photos taken; in the photo from 1959, Cricket Lodge, I see Sally in the top row, me in the second row, and Lynn and Denise in the third row, flanked by our counselors Shawnee and Woody. Campers were required to write home while we rested. Sally and I both wrote to Grandmother, too, expressing our gratitude for sending us there. I never slept at rest time, but Sally always conked right out for an hour or so. After resting, the counselors doled out our candy. Everybody brought candy to Shady Lawn; it was a tradition. Sally and I always loaded up on candy to bring to camp; sometimes our candy stash would have shrunk measurably even before we got to camp if it has been in our closet for more than a few days. If a camper ran out of candy or was a newbie and hadn't brought any, there was always a box of some stale leftovers called Camp Candy that counselors would give out. We called it Cramp Candy, which we thought was just hilarious.

Horseback riding was the highlight of our long summer days at Shady Lawn Farm. Campers were put in groups according to their riding skill. Ring was for the littlest campers and the girl with Down's syndrome. Goldie was big and fat and the gentlest of horses and didn't seem to mind going around in circles, hence the name of that class, Ring. Another group called Range rode horses in a big arena. Most of us were in Trail, which was a long line of horses, nose to tail, following a dusty trail along the Stanislaus River. Old Uncle Joe rode at the front of the line, followed by his grandson Jody, a teenager most of the girls had a crush on. Uncle Joe would yell, "Trot your horses" or "Canter your horses," and the horses would surge ahead at the sound of his voice. At the end of every two-week session, there was a horse show, on the day parents came to pick up their kids. Ribbons were awarded, and after a couple of years of getting thirds and seconds, I was so proud to get a blue one, for first place, in the Colt class, riding a two-year-old pinto gelding called Patches. My scrapbook contains the ribbons I won in those horse shows. By that time, I was old enough to have earned the right to be one of the kids who helped bridle and saddle the horses just after dawn. My heart was full when I walked up the dirt road between the cornstalks in the fields to the stables under a pink sky, amid the sweet smell of hay and horses and leather. One year while saddling, a horse stepped on my foot, and when I pulled it out, my big toenail was ripped off. I was only wearing tennis shoes. Fortunately, said the camp nurse, I was up-to-date on my tetanus shots. She cut a hole in my tennis shoe to accommodate the bandage that I had to wear for the rest of my summer. The next year, Mom bought Sally and me proper cowboy boots for camp.

Peter and I were in love for almost a whole year after we met at camp, though I don't recall ever speaking a word to him. Love is a fragile thing when you're twelve, and you dare not do anything that might collapse it.

I first noticed him at the camp's pool, where he was diving off the diving board with a group of boys who were shouting and laughing and splashing and doing what all adolescent boys do when water and sun and girls are present. I flung out my towel on the hot cement next to my friend Mary and squinted into the sun where Peter stood on the diving board, silhouetted against the sky, his light brown hair slicked down and his blue trunks dripping. The sun behind him made his ears translucent. Mary gave him a wave; she said she knew him from last summer. Mary would grouse that she and her brother were "shipped off to camp" all summer long. Both Sally and I agreed we would have loved to be "shipped off", to be able to spend the whole summer at camp would not be a cause for resentment.

I could see that Peter had a really wide mouth with braces on his teeth. He paused on the end of the diving board, looked over at Mary and me, and dove into the water, yelling something that I couldn't quite make out as his head hit the water. He swam over to the ladder and hauled himself out, returning to the board and yelling again as his voice was quenched by the water. Finally, I could hear what he was yelling: "Red, white, and black." This was repeated dozens of times as not only Peter but also other boys took up the chant as they dove into the pool. I realized the significance of the red, white, and black: the colors of my bathing suit. Yikes!

Rumor swept the camp that Peter and I liked each other. Though we had opportunities to meet face to face, such as at the pool, at the benches during announcement time, in the Craft House, in the dining hall, or at the barn where we helped get horses ready for the trail rides, for the rest of our session, we managed not to eat at the same table, sit on the same bench, or cross paths at the barn. All communication was done long distance—he stared at me from afar until I looked over to him, at which time he would look away. And vice versa. Messages were passed via go-betweens, my

---

friend Mary and his friend Johnny: "see ya at the pool" or "see ya at the swings." But once there, we both failed to get close enough to even touch. There probably was a reason for this, besides the fear of saying the wrong thing or having a zit on one's face. Peter *may* have been shorter than I was. I strongly suspected this; I had been the tallest girl in my class the previous year. He must have feared it as well. The only logical thing to do to perpetuate our romance was not to get close enough to confirm. Across the pool, on a horse, sitting on the lawn, who could be sure of a person's height?

On my last day of camp that year, Sally and I were dragging our suitcases across the lawn to our parents' car when Peter's friend Johnny came running up to me with a piece of paper. "It's Peter's address. Will you write to him?" gasped Johnny. I could see Peter standing in the shadows near the dining hall. "Sure," I said. I wrote my address on the bottom of the paper and ripped it in half. Johnny ran back to deliver my address to Peter, and they both waved. I waved hesitantly so I wouldn't raise Mom's and Dad's eyebrows and be subjected to their teasing all the way home. Sally knew but had her own crush on a boy named Jack. She wouldn't have wanted to be teased about that either. She and I actually never discussed boys; we respected each other's privacy.

Peter and I did write back and forth during the school year, dutifully marking our successes and failures, dance classes, riding lessons, home runs, and As on spelling quizzes. It was understood that the distance between his home in Berkeley and mine in Menlo Park was too vast to even attempt a "long distance" phone call, much less a visit.

On Valentine's Day, a letter from Peter arrived on the usual blue stationery. The envelope felt lumpy. When I opened it, I found a heart-shaped pendant taped to the letter. Mom said it wasn't "real," but the gold tone was as real as the sun and moon to me. The letter was reserved, formal, as always, but was signed "Love, Peter." When I wrote to thank him, I, too, signed off with "Love." I wondered, *Did this mean we were lovers?*

I thought about Peter constantly; he was a vague, faraway figure in my shadows. I sped my bike home from school to retrieve the mail, and I sometimes walked around the house with a letter in my pocket, feeling its edges, before reading it at my desk in our room. I saved every one of his letters in a shoebox under my bed. I often sat at the piano, looking out the window instead of practicing. Mom accused me of "moping." I probably was, but also, I had no talent for the piano unlike Sally, who had inherited a full array of musical gifts from Dad and Gma.

The end of Peter's and my love was sealed when a month before we were to go back to camp came the news that Peter and I could not share the same two-week session because of his family's plan to vacation in Wyoming. He would go to camp, but later in the summer, and our paths would not cross. I was in anguish for weeks, but there it was. That summer I went to camp and connected again with Mary, and for us, there were other boys, ones who would sit next to us and talk. By the end of the summer, Peter's and my letters dwindled and, after a time, ended. I kept the heart-shaped necklace for a while, even into high school. But finally, it, too, slipped away as first loves usually do.

★ ★ ★

My Gma was really one of a kind. When I was ten, I took the train to stay with her in Hollywood during Easter vacation. She had decamped from Klamath Falls to Hollywood a few years after my grandfather died in 1946. Sally was miffed at not being invited. But Gma never tried to conceal the fact that I was her favorite; she told everybody. This annoyed Mom, who muttered that it was poor form to favor one grandchild over others, but she let me go. Gma probably knew what was poor form, but she did as she pleased most of the time, and I was the exalted one, the lucky recipient of her attentions.

Gma had a system for remembering. She'd taken a course in memory improvement, in which you first memorize the system's ten key words: *hat*, *hen*, *ham*, *hare*, *cup*, *shoe*, *cow*, *ape*, *woods*, and I forgot the tenth one. The system was you would then use these words to associate with whatever was on your list to remember. She was determined to teach me the system; she really believed in it. "Let's say you need these things at the store," she'd start off as I groaned silently. "Butter, Cheerios, hamburger buns, and toilet paper. So you take the first one, butter, and figure out a way to associate that with the first keyword, which is *hat*." She'd continue, conjuring up some relationship between improbable items, as if it all made perfect sense. Butter-hat? I'd puzzle, and she would continue, "Now the second item, Cheerios, make a connection with the second keyword, *hen*." *The hen laid a Cheerio?* I'd wonder, and so on. "You see, it's all done by association, and you'll never need a written shopping list again."

The system taxed my imagination far too much to relate butter with hats and cereal with hens, though if a hat or ham just happened to be on your shopping list, it was a cinch, or shoes, and it wasn't a stretch to imagine toilet paper on your shoe or how it could be associated with a cow (I don't find it so onerous to jot down needed items on a shopping list that I keep in the kitchen). Gma also insisted I memorize all the state capitals and all the US presidents in order, quizzing me endlessly whenever she visited.

Mom and Dad sang, "Hollywood, da da da da da, Hollywood," on the way to the train station. It wasn't until I lived in Los Angeles years later that I finally saw what they were making fun of: Hollywood was a mecca of dreams and phoniness and movie glitz, all of which my Gma took seriously. She called her adoptive home Down There when she visited with us in Northern California. This embarrassed me no end because my mother had recently explained about menstruation and related topics, referring to the mysterious pubic region as Down There. Sally and I sat on our twin beds, clutching our bears for comfort, while Mom made her quiet revelations.

It was hot in Hollywood that spring, 1955, but Gma lived on a street lined with the sycamores that gave the street its name. Her duplex, or apartment as she called it, was cool. The sycamores arched their long branches all the way over the street, shading the homes on it from the dry southwestern heat. Her place was a Spanish-tiled stucco, small but ample for a widowed lady. I guess any living quarters that weren't large and grand, with verandas, a center staircase, an attic, and full basements like the homes she had lived in in Klamath Falls, seemed to her just an apartment. Her Cadillac was parked on a driveway that was two cement strips with grass down the middle.

During that week's visit, I saw Gma on her own turf, how she lived day to day. Her dim front room was crammed with dark, heavy furniture and several layers of Persian carpets. Crocheted doilies draped over the arms of chairs and sofas. Spread over the piano bench was what she called a camel saddlebag, scratchy red and orange wool with long tassels. Gma was pleased when I sat down at the piano, even if it was just to play "Chopsticks" or "Country Gardens," really the only songs I knew. The Venetian blinds were usually closed, making the room even murkier. Her closets were full of suits, coats, furs, and hats and rows of high heels. She even had high heels on her bedroom slippers. She claimed that years of wearing only high heels had shortened the tendons in the back of her heels, so she had to continue to wear heeled shoes for the rest of her life, even around her apartment. *Mm-hmm.*

I observed her beauty regimen, including morning makeup, wig selection, and a turn on the Exercycle bike in her kitchen. I got on it once, and the rocking back and forth made me seasick, even after she turned it down to Slow. I saw that she had gotten contact lenses. "Glasses, especially bifocals, make me look old!" she said. She pried up her eyelids, and it looked like it must hurt. I couldn't understand why she would want to dig those tiny circles out of her eyes every day; I couldn't watch the ritual after that. But there wasn't much Gma wouldn't do to perpetuate her youth. I had overheard my parents discussing Gma's plastic surgery—a face-lift and, even earlier, a nose job. "She might have been the first non-movie star in Hollywood to have a face-lift," my mother said. My father remarked that it couldn't have been easy to arrange the nose job, what with the war on and all. Mom muttered that "other people had the war under control so SHE could concentrate on her looks." Mom was fond of Gma, but still . . .

Gma's teeth were new too. At night, they rested in a glass in the bathroom, smiling ghoul-like in a neon blue solution. I brushed my teeth with extra vigor under their gaze. "My grandmother has fake teeth," I announced to my teacher later, knowing that the words *fake* and *false* meant the same thing. Now we call them dentures.

During my visit, Gma did her best to keep a ten-year-old amused. We went to movies: Lucille Ball and Desi Arnaz in *The Long, Long Trailer.* I laughed at Lucy when she fell in the mud. We visited the La Brea Tar Pits where we saw the bones of saber-toothed tigers and giant mastodons with great curved tusks. The displays showed these prehistoric monsters resurrected and preserved, and I wondered why so many animals hadn't figured out, after seeing others struggle and sink, that they shouldn't step into the goo. We went to the Farmer's Market on Fairfax Avenue. I bought a postcard to send home, a postcard with citrus groves that reportedly grew in the region, but all I'd seen were streets and cars and houses and large buildings. After our lunch, I waited on the corner with a bag of fresh dates, waiting for Gma to bring her car around. I saw her drive up in her Cadillac, so I stepped close to the curb and reached out for the door handle. But somehow, she hadn't seen me in the crowd, and she swept right around the corner, her front tire running over the tip of my shoe. The second time she came around, she saw me, and I got in and said nothing; what would be the point? My Gma just did things like that.

Though I knew Disneyland was under construction somewhere in that teeming Los Angeles area, it wasn't quite ready for the public yet, and in any case, amusement parks with Dumbo and Mickey Mouse and rollercoaster rides were not my Gma's style. We drove downtown to Olvera Street, went out Wilshire and Sunset Boulevard, and saw the tall white letters spelling out *Hollywood* on a hillside. We shopped—Gma loved Robinson's, The May Company, and Bullock's. But she rarely actually bought anything.

She gave me a home permanent and then took me to her beauty shop to have a professional set. We were both still blowing our noses from the ammonia fumes of the fresh permanent solution as we walked in, but to my surprise, Gma proceeded to tell the beautician that I had naturally curly hair, as if the woman couldn't smell the reek of Toni solution on my wet hair. Actually, I did have curly hair, but apparently, it wasn't curly enough for Gma.

We went out to eat often; Gma wasn't much of a cook. One night, she said we were going out to a special dinner. She had told me all the biggest movie stars in the world lived right here in her city. We got all dolled up. Gma was swathed in swishy black taffeta, topping the ensemble with a fur stole and a tiny hat with a veil that looked like a spiderweb. A brooch was pinned to her lapel, and earrings hung desperately from each pale stretched earlobe. Her wrists clanked with bracelets. A fog of perfume followed Gma everywhere, so pungent as to be almost visible, like the Air Wick that my father sprayed in the bathroom at home.

She had bought me a frilly pink voile and organza dress with lots of petticoats that my mother would groan over later, saying it was murder to iron. "You've got to look like somebody, honey," Gma said, and I think she wanted me to look like Shirley Temple (I had the hair, for sure), even though little Shirley was already a wife and mother by the mid-1950s. A decade later, when everybody looked like nobody, in jeans, sweatshirts, and long stringy hair, she shook her head and sighed. By then, at least I had filled out, and at Thanksgiving or Christmas, she'd say to me, "Stand up and show everybody your figya," and I would twirl, scarlet faced, as she clucked her approval.

Gma took my beauty regimen under her tutelage, with such wisdom as "Don't eat standing up, you'll have heavy thighs," and "Don't rub underneath your eyes, you'll break all the little bones there, and you'll have bags." She advised me to postpone wearing fingernail polish until my nails had a chance to "develop." "And don't scratch your head in public. People will think you have cooties." Cooties were not defined.

16

We drove down Wilshire in Gma's white fin-tailed Cadillac to our dinner. For years, she bought a new white Cadillac every year until she ran low on funds and then claimed that she would keep her car because she didn't like the new styles. I wondered if we were going to The Brown Derby, which I had read about in *Modern Screen* magazine. Big stars like Fernando Lamas and Lana Turner went there. Gma steered around the palm tree–lined streets until she nosed the Caddy into a parking place big enough for a bus—she never managed to get the hang of parallel parking. She checked herself in the mirror, smiling wide with teeth bared like a chimp, and turned to me and pinched me hard on both cheeks—to give me some color, she said. We walked along the sunburned street, me rubbing my cheeks and squirming in the scratchy organza dress that seemed to hold in the heat radiating up from the pavement. Gma's high heels popped like popcorn on the sidewalk. She paused at a big picture window to adjust her fur stole, and I could see directly above us a huge blue and white windmill, its arms revolving slowly around, and a sign saying Van de Kamp's.

"Here we are," she announced, pushing through the door. She said this was her favorite place, a sort of upscale cafeteria. She grabbed a plastic tray and headed for the stack of plates and began loading up, moving regally through the line, chatting with the employees, and waving to some acquaintances already at their tables. I pushed my tray past heat lamps pointed at a huge hunk of roast beef hanging from chains like a tortured prisoner. Farther on were hams as big and round as basketballs, corned beef swimming in a peppercorn bath, mashed potatoes, and green beans in square steel holding tanks. Three vats of salad dressing, white, orange, and oily clear, sat in front of long rows of tossed greens that reminded me of the lettuce fields I had seen from the train windows around Salinas. At the end of the lineup, before the cash register, were rows of small dishes containing pudding or cubes of lime green or red Jell-O. There were also squares of mahogany cake with perfectly combed frosting and lemon meringue pie with brown beads of sweat on top. Behind stood small dark-haired ladies in hairnets who praised our choices, replacing plates as soon as they were taken, like a factory assembly line.

Gma paid, and we sat down at one of the Formica tables. Gma composed her plate and cup of decaffeinated Sanka (I thought it smelled like old socks), positioned her napkin and silverware, and said grace. After saying

---

grace, she then began her usual dining-out ritual: she'd dunk each piece of silverware into her water glass and scrub it off vigorously with her napkin. She claimed restaurants didn't get the silverware clean enough. What was puzzling to me about this was that, as she then ate her meal, she proceeded to drink the dunk water, apparently oblivious to whatever grease, bits of rice, or parsley that may have been floating like flotsam in her glass. As we ate, I looked around in vain for movie stars, but Gma leaned forward to whisper that some of the waiters and busboys and even the ladies behind the counters were future stars just waiting to be discovered.

We went to Gma's church on Wednesday night and on Sunday morning. The Christian Science church was a cornerstone of her social life. Another activity was going to the Veteran's Hospital, where she played the piano and sang and played cards with men who had fought in wars. She skipped her veteran's visit while I was there, but she really was keen to show me off at her church. At the Wednesday night service, parishioners gave "testimony" pertaining to their faith. Gma stood up and told the congregation how when my father was a little boy, he was standing too close to the fireplace, and his night clothes caught fire. But because of her prayers, she told the congregation, my father didn't have a burn on him. Her faith was unshakable. A big sign hanging on the church wall said God Is Love. That was the one takeaway I got from Christian Science.

While I sometimes was embarrassed by her flamboyance, at church, I felt proud hearing her strong soprano voice vibrating alongside me as we sang "Onward Christian Soldiers." I knew she occasionally was invited to sing a solo and had, as a young woman, studied to be an opera singer with the San Francisco Opera Company. She told me how she took voice lessons with "the best voice teachers in the West." She was the featured vocalist in the Oregon Building at the 1915 Pan Pacific Exposition. After that, she left her new husband in Klamath Falls to go to San Francisco to take opera lessons, understudy some roles, audition, practice, and wait for her big chance. She sang in churches all over San Francisco and Oakland during that time as well. She told me once that if my grandfather had only believed in her dream enough to be her manager, she could have had the excitement of a life as an opera star. But she didn't begin to train seriously until she was thirty-five, when she was probably too old to launch an opera career. Besides, my grandfather, AJ, refused, according to my father, "to get involved with all those fairies." AJ was a lumberman, one of three partners, and the general manager of the Big Lakes Box Company. He had less than no interest in opera. Gma finally came home to Klamath Falls in 1918; had her only child, my father, in 1919; and settled down to be a wife and mother. She devoted her musical talents to her hometown. She taught voice and piano and organized community music performances.

Even at ten years old, I knew the subject of Gma's age was taboo. Gma and her sister, my aunt Agnes, both lied about their ages, but Gma had even more reason to do so: her husband, AJ, had been ten years younger than her. At family gatherings, when there was mention of something that she should have been too young to remember, she would change the subject or stride into the kitchen to help with the dishes.

After AJ's death in 1946 and my father and family moving to Menlo Park, she headed for Hollywood. She was a perfect candidate for the land of dreams and make-believe. At some point in the 1950s or 1960s, she told my father she had lost her birth certificate, which may have been true, but it was more likely that it had been disposed of so she could arrange to get a new one and lop twenty years off her age. (She only needed to cut ten years to even it up with her deceased husband, but she chose to shave another ten just for good measure.) She had read in the paper that you could get some sort of form verifying your birth by getting a close relative to sign an affidavit. Aunt Agnes was only too pleased to verify Gma's new birthdate, and naturally, Gma returned the favor, so both ladies were born again, right there in the Los Angeles County Courthouse. Gma's new birthdate was 1900 (I saw it on her driver's license), and Agnes's was 1901. They had been actually born, the first time, in 1880 and 1881, coming west to Oregon from Tennessee when they were about five and six. Gma was insulted when I asked her if they came by covered wagon. "We came on the train!" she huffed. I wondered, *Had the railroad even been extended all the way to Oregon by then?*

My father, who had accompanied them to the courthouse, told his uncle Bill how disgusted he had been that his mother and aunt had pulled this scam, but since he wasn't born until 1919 and had no written proof of the tightly held truth, he had to sit and grind his teeth until the affidavits were filed. Bill said, "All I know is that I was born in 1900, and when I was a little boy, your mother was already a grown-up woman!"

The last time I saw my Gma, it was 1969. By then, I was living with a friend in Glendale and working downtown Los Angeles on Spring Street in the financial district. Gma liked to take me to dinner at another one of her favorite haunts, Manning's, a "cafe" according to her, which was ever so much more refined and cosmopolitan than a mere coffee shop. She always called the staff Honey or Dear. The waitress set down our plates: two patty melts flanked by perfect snowballs of cottage cheese. We were dieting. "You don't recognize me, do you, honey?" she said as she swished her fork in her water glass and worked the tines with her napkin. "I usually come here with different men," she said, and the Honey who was waiting on us nodded numbly with a thin smile. I was mortified—Gma sounded like some kind of elderly escort, sort of like Mae West. She was, of course, talking about the veterans that she occasionally treated to a dinner out, but she was rather overly proud of herself at her age for being sought after by men of any sort. In addition to those, she had been "keeping company" occasionally with a man named Hal.

I looked into my plate with its gray planet of meat and its cottage cheese moon and tried to find it appealing. Gma wanted to meet because she was giving me her contract for a health club in Hollywood. It was a three-year membership that she was way too old for, but the gym had been too glad to take her money when she first signed up. Despite the contract's fine print forbidding any transfer of membership and in a rare concession to her age, Gma had finally convinced the gym's management that she couldn't continue and to allow me to take it over. After we talked about that and Honey had refilled her Sanka cup, Gma's smile drooped, and I noticed her dry red hands were shaking. I knew she wouldn't admit to being unwell; her Christian Science faith denied sickness the way she denied aging. Her floury cheeks were paler than usual. She told me she had fallen down last week in front of her building. She had moved to a multistory building that housed primarily senior citizens, just a few streets over from where she had lived for twenty plus years on Sycamore. She loved that there was an upholstered bench to sit on in the elevator, and when she sat on the bench as we rode up to her floor, she recited her special prayer for the elevator.

I didn't know what to say when she said she had fallen. I was still in my mid-twenties, far too young to understand the difficulties and the horrors of aging, the fear of imminent death. What was the big deal to fall down? I fell now and then on a carpet edge or a crack in the pavement, and it didn't mean anything. When you become elderly, falling is treacherous. A broken hip can end your mobility and lead to pneumonia and death. And of course, she saw it as a sign of her own vulnerability, her own mortality.

I looked at her, and instead of my proud, puffed-up, stiff-corseted, yet loving Gma, I saw a small, soft, frail person who had spent so much time and energy and money trying to be newer than she was. I saw somebody who made unwise decisions over furs and cars and giving jewelry to small children. I saw her dreams for my personal success measured by how I looked (but she might have gotten it right about the heavy thighs) and how well I remembered shopping lists with *hat, hen, ham, hare, shoe, cow, ape,* and *woods* and how nicely I could recite the presidents in order. I knew her dreams; she was an opera star who hadn't been discovered—yet.

Before we left the café, we visited the ladies' room where Gma took out her false teeth and rinsed them under the tap, her mouth all caved in. She whipped off her curly apricot-colored wig and gave it a shake. Her real hair lay in thin white wisps across her pink skull like the mare's tail clouds that streak the sky.

In a few months, Gma would be dead, and I wish I had talked to her more about her family; she was proud to trace her lineage back to Light-Horse Harry Lee and Robert E. Lee. Her father was Joseph Pearson Lee, who fought in the Civil War with a Tennessee regiment, Company H (he was the frequently mentioned Captain Lee in the Civil War memoir *Company Aytch* by Sam Watkins.) I would have liked to know more about what he thought about that terrible war and why he then brought his family west to Oregon where he homesteaded briefly, ran a hotel, and later served as a county assessor. I would have asked her about those lost years of her youth around 1900 (her *real* twenties) or about her scandalizing the staid neighborhood in Klamath Falls (I heard this from Dad) when she strapped on some skis and skied down the hill from her house on High Street to downtown during the Depression. Apparently, married ladies of a certain age didn't do things like that in Klamath Falls. There was so much more I wanted to find out—why was her brother never mentioned?—but she died one evening in her Hollywood apartment. The manager of her building found her, all dressed up, sitting in a chair, wearing a mink stole, ready to go out.

When Mom and Dad went Down There to close out Gma's apartment, a number of her friends called with sympathy. Mom said several of them, after a respectful pause, asked, "How old was she, anyway?" Gma would have been proud. Mom said her driver's license said she was sixty-nine. That was true, wasn't it? Gma was laid to rest peacefully at Forest Lawn Cemetery, among the stars. She's buried a couple of rows down from Clark Gable.

★ ★ ★

I started high school at Menlo-Atherton High in 1959. All my Oak Knoll friends were there (we'd been together since second grade), so I didn't feel overwhelmed by the sprawling campus. There were kids from Hillview and Encinal elementary schools and intriguing black students from Ravenswood across the freeway. One of them was a girl named Ellie who was in my PE class. She wasn't tall but had the best vertical jump in the class and always seemed to score baskets from the free-throw line. She had a brother named Nat, who was on the track team.

I met a new friend, Pam, in my Spanish class. Pam lived within walking distance of Cotton Place, though she had gone to the neighboring elementary school, Hillview. We began to spend time at either our house or hers. She was the top student in Spanish, and I was right behind. I was determined to speak Spanish as well as she did.

One Friday night, I was sleeping over at Pam's house. Pam's older sister Carol, a senior, had invited some friends of hers from the track team at Menlo-Atherton, and we were all sitting around in the basement of their house. Someone was playing the guitar. We could hear the wooden creaking from Pam's parents walking around upstairs. Her parents were what we might have called hippies, though the term had not yet entered our lexicon. Pam had told me her parents encouraged her and Carol to socialize with black students at Menlo-Atherton to "widen their view of the world," as they put it.

Carol and Rico had been seeing each other for a few months. Rico was an outstanding athlete in football, basketball, and track. Among the dozen or so other dark faces in that basement was my PE classmate Ellie's brother Nat. He and Rico were both track stars. They won at the high hurdles, the long jump, and the sprints. A boy named Darnell shifted around the circle to sit near Pam. Nat said hello, and after a while, he sat behind me on the cool cement floor. Suddenly, he plunged both hands down the front of my jeans, close to the top of my pubic hair. Down There! I was paralyzed and mute, and I still, to this day, don't know why I just sat there, probably in a combination of embarrassment, fear, and bafflement. Nat was directly behind me; I couldn't even see his face. Should I have squawked and risked spoiling the quiet gathering? Should I have excused myself to go upstairs, risking interrogation from Pam's parents? I did nothing. The hands stayed where they were, and they didn't stray further until eventually the boys went home. I said nothing to Pam either. Of course, I would understand later that my lack of resistance was tantamount to encouragement. Mom never mentioned such a scenario, and I was too embarrassed to confide in her or anyone.

The next weekend, Pam and I waited on the corner near my house for Darnell and Nat to pick us up. It was a Saturday morning in late spring, cool with a promise of warmth later in the day. Pam had on new shorts and a white middy-style blouse with a navy-blue tie. I thought my old beige shorts and pink T-shirt looked drab next to her. We stood, brushed by the morning light, shifting our weight from one leg to the other, speaking to each other in Spanish as we often did. I was still her greatest rival for the top spot in our Spanish class. We used Spanish as a kind of code, infuriating non-Spanish-speaking people around us who wondered what kind of secrets or snide remarks we were making.

We waited in the spring light, clamping our elbows into our pelvic bones, studying our shoes, scanning the sky. Pam leaned against an olive-green bulk mailbox and unwrapped a stick of Doublemint gum. She propped one leg out at an angle and bent the other knee until her foot was flat against the mailbox. I thought she looked sexy that way, her shiny blonde hair falling over her face like a veil. The liquidambar trees were just leafing out, their bronze leaves big as baseball mitts. The smell of wisteria floated from a basket weave fence behind us. Across the street was the home of a guy at our school named Biff Mudd. Seriously.

Finally, a dusty Chevrolet chugged up to the corner. It was light green, probably shiny when it had been new, but now it was faded and dull, like the color of our high school infirmary. Darnell's dark elbow hung over the passenger-side windowsill, and then he waved. I stood at the curb, nervous as a puppy, my face pink with shyness. Pam still stood propped against the mailbox, examining her nails. She could get away with things like that.

I sighed, envying her worldliness, her knowledge. I thought about all our talks, how, like her parents, she believed black people were equal, how we needed to give them all our support now that things were finally opening up for them. Rosa Parks had refused to go to the back of the bus a few years earlier, and Dr. Martin Luther King was exhorting black people to dream the dream of equality. We were aware that in the South, thousands of miles away but still in our own country, black people had separate water fountains and separate bathrooms and were denied entry to certain places, even though those places were public. *How unfair*, we thought. Why? There was none of that in Menlo Park, but it was true that no black people lived on our side of the freeway.

Pam admitted to having feelings for Darnell, but I didn't know how strong they might be. She knew he was crazy about her. I wasn't at all sure how I felt about Nat; I hardly knew him. He had called me at home twice during the week. We didn't really have much to say during those conversations. We were just two teens with a curiosity about each other, about anyone, really, of the opposite sex. I didn't know what my parents would have thought about him because I never told them a thing. I'd had my preteen romance with Peter from camp, and I'd had some crushes in seventh and eighth grade, but they were unrequited. One snaggle-toothed eighth grader told me that he liked me, but I was the unrequiter.

Today, we were going to the Pulgas Water Temple. Pam and Darnell climbed into the back seat of the car, and I settled into the front passenger seat with Nat. We drove up into the foothills decorated with spring blossoms. Pam and Darnell were kissing already. Nat kept glancing in his rearview mirror at them. He looked to me so unknowable, such a foreigner to my life thus far. The car was hazy with cigarette smoke, and jazz music poured softly from the radio. We drove into the hills of Woodside, the road lined with meadows of bright green and oaks offering hesitant new growth to the breeze that was as tender as baby's skin. We passed the stables where I used to take horseback riding lessons. A girl was coaxing her horse up to a jump, and I could hear the *thunk*, *thunk* of her booted heels against the horse's belly. My horsy days at Shady Lawn Farm suddenly seemed so long ago.

Nat turned the car into a gravel parking area flanked by fields brimming with yellow mustard grass. Tiny brown birds jumped off the wooden fence like gliders. A blackbird sporting orange epaulets sang a single note for the joy of it. Four gray granite obelisks guarded the entrance to the temple grounds. A sign announced we were at the Pulgas Water Temple, Terminus, Hetch Hetchy Aqueduct, San Francisco Water District. Pam's head peeked out of the tent she and Darnell had made out of his letterman's jacket to hide under during our drive. "*Tengo pulgas*," she squeaked, laughing, pulling the jacket back over her head.

Nat glared, not understanding our language. I explained that she said she had fleas (*pulgas*). Even my translation didn't mollify him as we both got out of the car and walked down an incline to the roaring water of the temple. Pam and Darnell remained in the car.

We crunched across the gravel. I looked back at the car, where heat waves were already dancing across its hood. Darnell's dark jacket disappeared. The roar of the water got louder as we walked down the slope to the edge of the long rectangular reflecting pool. The pool reflected slender cypresses that thrusted into the sky. As we got closer to the pool, it no longer looked so pure. I saw brown scum on the sides and floating algae. We neared the Greek columns where the water sounded like a swift mountain cataract and walked up the broad steps like concentric layers on a wedding cake. Ten fluted columns pushed into the sky from the circular thundering basin. Above was a round stone cap decorated with chiseled swags of fruits, vegetables, grains, and other bounty of the earth.

I gripped the cold edge with both hands and looked down into the cataclysm of water, just like Niagara Falls I imagined, the water frothing white and deafening ten feet below. I closed my eyes and imagined falling in, the force of the water pushing me, pummeling me like a powerful surf, my body helpless against the water. If I fell, would I be found weeks later, washed down the stone aqueduct into the reservoir, my face polished featureless like an agate in a constantly turning drum? I opened my eyes; the mist was a cool breath on my face. I could read the inscription on the bronze plaque on the rim, a Bible quotation from Isaiah: "I give waters in the wilderness and rivers in the desert to give drink to my people."

Nat and I turned away from the churning water and found a place to sit on the grass near the reflecting pool. Bees moved over the grass, humming in the clover blossoms. An old dowager of an oak whose skirts reached almost to the ground gave us her shade. Nat stretched out, easing a hip into the grass and propping his wide shoulders up on an elbow. His muscles moved pantherlike underneath his dark taut skin. I sat a few feet away, too conscious of myself, my legs tightly curled underneath me. He talked, nervous and offhand, teasing and suggestive. He yanked up clumps of grass and threw them at my legs. He smoked a cigarette. I watched the smoke trail up through the oak leaves, wondering what to say that wouldn't make me seem an eejit. I had my notions of love and romance, chivalry, and fairy tales. Did I mention I always had my nose in a book? I was not so sure about being here right now . . .

Nat smashed out his cigarette and rolled over to put his head in my lap. My heart thumped. I hadn't even held hands or kissed a boy, and the only male hands on me until last week in the basement had been at dance class. (Actually, because of my height, I sometimes had to *be* the boy because more girls than boys had signed up for dance lessons.) I never did dance well because of that. Nat's wooly hair looked like broccoli, green tinted by the oak leaf shade. He stroked my arm, my body tingled; his hands were dry as chalk. Bees buzzed even louder, and I started to sweat.

I broke the spell. I tried to stand. I felt out of time, out of place. I couldn't let myself get carried away. I was fourteen; this was crazy. "Let's go," I said too quickly; I was afraid, afraid of the bulge in his pants, his smooth whispering. Now he was behind me, pressing his hips into mine, rocking, murmuring. I feared the sweetness, the wanting, the not wanting. I closed my eyes against it. It would be so easy to be pulled along like the relentless flow of water, be part of the ancient rituals of mankind and nature, but I thought, guiltily, I'm just a kid. This is not for me this time, this day, this person. I jerked myself away and walked toward the car.

"Why'd ya come here then?" Nat asked, his voice now harsh. "You prejudice. I bet you let white boys do it to you all night long. If you really for equality like you say, you let me do it to you!" Somehow, this emotional extortion sounded well-practiced. I understood; I needed to submit to him to prove I weren't prejudiced. Acceptance and inclusiveness weren't enough? I couldn't look at him; I hated him. He grabbed my arms and pressed me tightly against the cement retaining wall. I turned my face away from his dragon mouth. I was profiled against the emery-rough wall like an Egyptian bas-relief. He pushed his tongue into my mouth. One arm pinned me against the wall, and the other dove into my shorts like he had in Pam's basement. This time, his fingers found my hot folds. He leaned on me and pushed, now one hand over my mouth so I couldn't yell; who would hear anyway with the pounding water? I yelled, "Stop, you're hurting me!" Then I heard some kids running down the path to the water feature.

Nat looked around and stepped back. I crumpled to the grass as if my backbone were spaghetti. I covered my face with my hands and brought my knees to my chest. At first, I felt humiliated. Something shameful had just happened, for which I was so hopelessly unprepared, my knowledge so imperfect and shrouded in myth. And my romantic view of love had nothing to do with the carnality of what had just happened. Sex was still a mystery, and now I felt shocked and embarrassed. But also now I felt something like an accomplishment, just as when a year later, I would stagger out of the gas station bathroom after smoking my first cigarette, and I could cross that off my list of things to experience.

We walked to the car; Nat trailed behind me. I began to feel lighter, relieved; it was over. An initiation of sorts. In time, I would see that Nat and I used each other for practice. Also, in time, I would realize that I was lucky I wasn't raped. Now I wanted to go home and make cookies and play with our dog. I saw Pam and Darnell still in the back seat, laughing and tickling each other. Pam's blonde hair glinted in the sunlight. Darnell hummed to the song on the radio, his big brown paw splayed out on the whiteness of Pam's thigh. Pam and I didn't say a word then, nor did we ever later discuss our relationships with these boys. There were just some topics you didn't discuss, or didn't know how, even with your closest friend. I am one of those people who keep secrets.

Nat drove us back down the road, past the stables where the same girl was still urging the same horse over the jump. As we sailed past, I saw the girl and the horse arch fluidly over the bar and touch soundlessly to earth.

★ ★ ★

That summer, 1960, Dad changed jobs, and we moved from Menlo Park to the East Bay as soon as school was out after my freshman year of high school at Menlo-Atherton. We moved to a small town called Alamo, between Danville and Walnut Creek. We went from the warm and sunny Menlo Park and its "Mediterranean" climate to an area my uncle Dave and aunt Sally (who lived on the coast) would later dub "Death Valley." Temperatures in Alamo usually moved up to the three figures early in summers and stayed there for months. Our Death Valley (actually the San Ramon Valley) was long and narrow, with Walnut Creek at the north end and Dublin at the south. Highway 21 connected the towns, cutting through rolling green (and golden) hills dotted with grazing cattle and horses, oak trees, and groves of walnut trees. The house my parents bought was set on a lot of an acre and a third, shaded by a grove of huge walnut trees. A barn and corral (and a horse!) were located behind the three-car garage, and there was a separate garden shed.

The white wood-framed house was bigger than our Menlo Park house, which had been plenty roomy for a couple with two teenagers, two grade-schoolers, and assorted pets, but now we had a front porch running across the front, a side patio, a second story with three bedrooms, and a sleeping porch. The house had been built in the 1940s and needed some work.

When we first moved in, a wooden arch stretched across the driveway like the one in Rock Hudson's Texas ranch in the movie *Giant*. Mom labeled it "tacky," and she would know; she was from Texas. I thought it added a little country charm, but my opinion did not count; the arch was soon demolished. My dream of having a horse was also demolished when Mom declared that the horse (belonging to a neighbor) that was temporarily living in the attached barn and corral would soon be evicted and, to my great disappointment, would never be replaced by a horse of our own. Mom was adamant that she didn't want flies in her kitchen. The barn was torn down after a few months, but the corral remained where my brother burned leaves and trash every week in an old fifty-five-gallon drum. Dad planted a vegetable garden in that well-fertilized corral area, yielding tomatoes, zucchini, corn, peppers, basil, dill, and pumpkins. I ate tomatoes, warm, sharp, and juicy, when it was my turn to water the vegetables with a hose. Dad grew enormous pumpkins by removing all blossoms on the vine but one so he could enter them in the annual pumpkin contest at his favorite tavern. His morbidly obese pumpkins usually won, if he could get them into the bed of his pickup intact.

Twice a year, a man came to our property and pulled a corkscrew-looking apparatus behind his tractor, a process called "disking," which plowed under the weeds that grew under the walnut trees. In the fall, sharecroppers came with huge white tarps and harvested the walnuts and gave us a few boxes. We shucked off the moist green hulls until our hands turned black, and we laid the nuts in the sun to dry.

Inside the house, Mom, Sally, and I steamed layers and layers of old wallpaper off the plaster walls. The rented steamer sighed and burbled while I held it to the wall, one section at a time, and the rooms filled with the smell of wet paper. After a thorough drenching, you had to scrape off each new layer with a broad scraper. The previous owners had just papered over old wallpaper rather than strip it off. Mom was having none of that; she decreed that the walls would be stripped and painted. We stripped the entry hall, living room, kitchen, service porch, dining room, and the downstairs bedroom belonging to my parents. Note to self: Don't be seduced by pretty wallpaper. Paint walls instead. Carpet was installed in the living room, and rules were established forbidding passage across the carpet—from the front door to the kitchen, you had to dogleg down a hall and enter the brand-new family room that had transformed an old screened-in porch. The family room with its easy care linoleum floor held the grand piano, banquette seating, lots of built-in storage paneled in white-washed knotty pine, and a brick indoor barbecue that occupied center stage, particularly at Thanksgiving or Christmas when Dad loved to watch the turkey turn slowly on the spit. What had been a window from the kitchen to the former porch now became a pass-through, and what had been a bay window became the buffet.

Upstairs in the children's domain were three bedrooms and two baths; Rob had his own bath, and Sally, Anne, and I shared the other bath. Once again, I shared a bedroom and walk-in closet with Sally; Anne had her own bedroom. But we all slept on the sleeping porch, lined with single beds. It got almost cool enough by bedtime that you could sleep. Dad installed a rattly swamp cooler which sometimes had to be refilled with water when I got up in the night to go pee. Over the sound of the fan, most nights you could hear the peacocks up in the hills at the end of our street, sounding exactly like a lost child calling for help. Some nights the peacocks wandered down the street and hopped onto our roof, pecking at their own reflections in our second-story windows.

Twelve years later, the heat was fierce, too, on my wedding day in mid-July. The mercury soared to 109, and we sweltered at the rehearsal dinner the night before at the Danville Hotel. Bruce and I were married in a Catholic church in Danville by a priest who had reassured us earlier that despite my not being Catholic, "there are a number of successful mixed marriages in our parish." The priest also had a stutter which we hadn't detected at the brief meeting with him but was noticeable a couple of times during the ceremony. After the ceremony, the reception was at my parents' house, where there had been major changes in the landscaping and the addition of a pool since I had left home. The walnut orchard had been removed—Mom said they had some sort of blight—and had been replaced by California redwoods, ginkgos and flowering plums, magnolias and raphiolepsis, and lawns and brick walkways lined with white petunias. The garden shed was given over to pool equipment. Some of the wedding guests, including my heat-sensitive uncle Dave who braved Death Valley just for me, cooled off in the pool. I have a photo of Sally and Anne lifting their yellow bridesmaid dresses and wading into the pool's shallow steps like bright canaries in a bird bath.

The day three years after my wedding when Sally was killed was also a scorcher. We gathered in the house, pressed down with heat and grief. Rob, Anne, and I slumped in the family room, the shades drawn against the heat. There was not a thing to do; we were robots. Waves of people brought food; we ate mechanically. It was as if the house was filled with smoke; we wandered from room to room like red-eyed ghosts, each new arrival or phone call setting us off crying again. Police and newspaper reporters called. "She was in the wrong place at the wrong time," I heard Dad tell a reporter on the phone. None of us had a clue.

31

I can still see Sally that first summer we moved there. She would be an incoming freshman at San Ramon Valley High School in Danville, and I would be a sophomore. We were upstairs, organizing our closet, and she took a break to get the mail. We both corresponded faithfully with friends left behind in far-off Menlo Park. From the upstairs window, I saw her walking down the driveway, her blonde ponytail swinging. Heat rose from the asphalt in ripples. Mt. Diablo shimmered in the distance. She reached the metal mailbox and carefully opened the flap with just the minimum exposure of fingertip and thumb. She reached inside, grabbed the mail, and closed the flap with her elbow. She looked up and saw me and waved. She brought a letter upstairs, a letter from Nat. Sally had no idea about Nat. She wasn't the sort who would pry because she wouldn't want me to pry back about her relationships. In the life we had just moved away from, I had been at high school, and she had been in eighth grade, and I never spoke a word about my encounters with Nat. When she finally went downstairs to help Mom set the table, I opened and read the letter, full of Nat's undying love for me, his last letter to me as it turned out. I tore it into pieces and flushed it down the toilet.

Pam and I wrote back and forth a few times. Her family had moved away, too, that summer to Vermont. We lost touch. She and I had nothing to not talk about anymore.

The first few days at San Ramon Valley High, Sally and I ate lunch together in the girls' bathroom. Really. But soon enough, we each made our own friends from the classrooms and from the neighborhood. I had friends named Fran and Judy, and Sally had friends named Daphne and Jade. Sally loved singing in madrigals and aspired to be a cheerleader. I developed a spazzy, goofy persona; I had to be funny because I was never going to be one of the world's great beauties or intellects. I worked on the school newspaper, *Wolf Tracks*, and the annual yearbook. The teacher who advised the newspaper staff recommended me to an actual paid job my senior year: covering the sewer board meeting once a month. I felt right at home; I was comfortable with the board members, old guys in their red hunting hats who flicked their cigarette ashes into their pants cuffs when an ashtray wasn't handy like my dad did.

I was a decent student. I was reasonably socialized. I had the heart flutterings, the thrill of the dance in the gym, and movie dates. I held hands and kissed boys, sure of real loves and romance befitting a high schooler. I went away to college, the University of the Pacific in Stockton. I majored in journalism; I wanted to write. I wrote all four years for the college newspaper, the Pacific Weekly. We staffers called it the Pee Weakly.

★ ★ ★

My other grandmother, my mother's mother, was so practical, so good, so loving, so devout she could have been a saint. She was born in 1896 in Monterey Park, California, a suburb of Los Angeles that now is practically all Vietnamese. Her father, Harry Patton, was a newspaperman, and the family moved frequently whenever he accepted a new position up and down the West Coast. Grandmother was the youngest of four children: Joe, Clotilde, Irene, and Ysabel. She had been named for the Santa Ysabel tribe of Indians that lived in the region near where her family was living in the 1890s Her father, Harry, as a prominent citizen, was on the board of a mental hospital that was being built near San Bernardino. The board voted to name the hospital Patton State Hospital after him, and it bears his name to this day, as does the unincorporated area surrounding it. Patton State Hospital is a forensic psychiatric hospital in Patton, San Bernardino County, with a capacity of 1,287 inmates who have been committed by the judicial system. Its original name, The Southern California Asylum for the Insane and Inebriates, says it more poetically.

After Southern California, Harry headed north with his family to the city of Santa Cruz to go to work on the newspaper there. The family was there during the Great Quake of 1906, and Grandmother remembered as a ten-year-old walking down the stairs in their house and the staircase was wobbling. Later, she saw all the brick rubble on Pacific Avenue in downtown Santa Cruz. By the time she was a teen, the family lived in Bellingham, Washington. Her mother, Elizabeth, had died while Grandmother was in high school. Her father worked most of the time, except when he had what Grandmother called his "spells," which involved binge drinking. "I just ate my dinner and went to bed" was how she described her teens. Grandmother never took a drink in her entire life, probably thanks to the memory of those "spells." It seems ironic to me that the hospital for "inebriates" was named for my great-grandfather, the binge drinker.

For a time, Grandmother went to live with her sister Irene, who was married. At age seventeen, she entered the University of Washington and, like her two sisters before her, joined the Kappa Alpha Theta sorority. She came to the attention of fellow student Edward Clark Will, a member of Delta Tau Delta fraternity, who was majoring in petroleum engineering.

They graduated in May of 1917 and were married on Christmas Day. My grandfather Clark (he didn't go by his first name) served in the Navy during World War I, and that's the only day he could get leave. Grandmother told me for a time she worked in San Francisco for Wells Fargo Bank on Montgomery Street. She said in 1918, everyone wore flu masks on the streetcars.

Once Clark mustered out of his military service, he and Ysabel headed for oil country—Texas. During the 1920s and 1930s, they lived in Pampa, Amarillo, Wichita Falls, and Corpus Christi. Their two daughters, Patty (first name Elizabeth, but called Patty for her middle name, Patton) and Sarah Ellen (known as Sally), were a year apart just like Sally and me. Grandmother homeschooled them until college because most of the oil fields didn't have proper schools, in her opinion. Patty and Sally both went first to Principia, a Christian Science college in St. Louis, Missouri. They both transferred into the University of Texas in Austin, and both joined Kappa Alpha Theta sorority, natch.

Around that time, the 1930s, the rowing team from the University of Washington, my grandparents' alma mater, was winning races all over the United States and was going to the 1936 Olympics in Berlin. I can picture Clark and Ysabel, the two of them hovering over a staticky radio console in some gray wooden house out on the treeless Texas plains among the tumbleweeds and dust and armadillos. I can imagine them straining to hear the results of the races each day in faraway Germany and cheering for those boys when they won.

My mother, Patty, and my father, Joe, had met during the war and married in 1943 while he was stationed in Corpus Christi, Texas, where I was born in 1945. Aunt Sally (she hated the name Sarah Ellen so much she had it legally changed to Sally) married Dave, a Navy man a year or so later. After the war, Aunt Sally and Uncle Dave moved to San Gabriel, California, where eventually they adopted my cousins Mary and John.

Grandpop Clark retired from the oil business in the early 1950s, and he and Ysabel built a cabin on Orcas Island, Washington, and planned to enjoy retirement there. Grandpop loved fishing on his cabin cruiser, Stardust. But he died suddenly after only a couple of years into his retirement. As a devout Christian Scientist, Grandmother never discussed his or anyone's ill health or death (those were "errors"), so I don't know what he died of, except once Mom told me his blood pressure was the highest his doctor had ever seen. So Grandmother sold the cozy cabin with its view of Puget Sound and moved down to Menlo Park to be near us. She had a triplex built on Arbor Road, just a few blocks from our house on Cotton Place, and she lived on the income from the other two units. She became active in the Christian Science Church in Menlo Park.

It was nice to have Grandmother close by; she was so loved by all of us. We could ride our bikes over to her apartment. Sally and I watered her plants when she traveled. She grew guavas and Meyer lemons and made guava jelly and lemon marmalade. She had a cloisonne candy dish that made a faint ring when you tried surreptitiously to snag a piece of candy; Grandmother could hear it even from the kitchen and would call out, "Aha, not before dinner!" Another box was a music box that played the Christian Science hymn "O Gentle Presence" that we often sang at church. As gentle a presence as she was, she did have an iron will when it came to church—all four of us were expected to be dressed and ready when she drove over on Sunday morning to pick us up for church. Sally and I were usually dressed alike; it was easier to just buy (or sew; both Mom and Grandmother were dedicated seamstresses) two of the same dress. Gma sent us frilly ones at Christmas and Easter. My brother would cry; he hated getting dressed up, and I think he still does to this day. We were carted off to church, and Patty and Joe could have a blessed hour or so of quiet to have coffee and read the Sunday paper.

Grandmother decided to remain in Menlo Park after we moved to Alamo rather than move closer to where we had moved. She had put down roots (as a founding member of the shiny new Christian Science church in Menlo Park near Menlo-Atherton High.) After we moved to Alamo, Grandmother kept up the effort of taking us to church for a while, but the hour plus drive from Menlo Park and the lack of enthusiasm from all of us eventually took its toll on her willingness to devote practically her whole day to get us to church. For another thing, in our new hometown, there wasn't a proper church; the Christian Science congregation, such as it was, met in the Danville Women's Club, and it was a circle of folding metal chairs. The smallest children were in the kitchenette, and the rest of us, maybe twenty people, sat in the main room on those cold hard chairs, listening to one of the ladies drone on from the *Science and Health with Key to the Scriptures*. Somebody banged out a few hymns on an old upright piano. It could have been engaging, like being at a gathering of the Apostles, all full of the spirit. Instead, it was like a sewer board meeting. It was the longest hour of my week.

But even after she gave up driving over to our house every Sunday, Grandmother managed to visit us often on holidays and birthdays. She came when Sally was killed, and she came five years later when Dad died. By the time she was in her nineties, she was a calm and beatific presence at family gatherings, sometimes dozing, occasionally clasping our hands and smiling, in full possession of her faculties. She died at age ninety-four in her own apartment. She had given up her car, and her nephew (her sister Irene's grandson) Toby, who lived nearby, came to pick her up for church and found her.

I was bereft; I wanted to tell her about so many things. Just a couple of years later, we had a family reunion (called a Tub Thump) at Orcas Island, and I wanted so badly to tell her about it, so in keeping with her belief that there was no death, she was simply away, I wrote to her as if she were vacationing in the Bahamas.

Dear Grandmother,

It's been a while since you died, and I wanted to bring you up-to-date. I still miss you. We finally scattered your ashes off Orcas Island like you wanted. It took a whole year to coordinate everyone's schedules; cousin Mary had to work, I had to work, Mom had to have some radiation for breast cancer, but don't worry, it was just a tiny "error," and she's just fine. Anyway, John and his wife, Sue, also came up and stayed in that little trailer behind Harry's place, and the boys (she has had two more since you left us) ran around like little mule deer; they always seem to have the sniffles. Joan is still ill. You remember how she was so puny at the last Tub Thump? This time, Harry had to actually carry her through the woods to Bob and Marjorie's Quonset. He was about done in with the effort, but she seemed to perk up a bit and told some wry stories, always behind a veil of cigarette smoke.

Bob and Dorothy finally finished their place; it's now an architectural wonder! Bob's retired from the U of W, and they live on the island permanently. When we scattered your ashes, Mom and Dorothy, neither of them keen on boating, watched from their porch while we rowed out to the Peapods. Uncle Dave and Aunt Sally were arguing the whole way out there, making me wish I'd stayed on land too, but finally, we got there and said a prayer, not the Scientific Statement of Being, but the other one you made us memorize as kids. The ashes floated on the still water. The weather held beautifully for July; you know how unpredictable it can be!

We beached the boat on that little inlet below Bob's place, not the rocky beach below your old place, where you used to moor your cruiser, Stardust. I looked up to your old cabin, now owned by strangers, of course, and imagined you and Grandpop watching the shorebirds at dusk. The wildflowers were beautiful on that path that leads up from the beach, and sturdy vines twist all the way up (though Harry built some wooden steps, it still helps to grab a vine occasionally) Even though I was only about five or six when I was there as a kid, I still remember the berries, the sunburns, the pancakes, the deer, and the salmon that we caught off the back of Stardust. My favorite picture of Grandpop in my scrapbook is one of him on the boat, wearing his captain's hat. Anyway, Dave could have used some of Grandpop's boating expertise on this outing, but I guess fiberglass can be fixed. He must have been feeling the stress of being our skipper, despite having served in the Navy. I can't really blame him; several bulky women in a tippy rowboat is a grave responsibility. He took a long walk by himself until dinner.

Thurm, the neighbor, came over that night and helped the boys with fireworks. Indians sell all types of fireworks out of flimsy stands as if they were selling lemonade; it is illegal in California now, but it's fine with just about everybody in Washington, though it seems to me there's just as much fire danger. The evening was so still and so dark, and the fireworks lit up the sky like jewels on black velvet. The moon was a golden scimitar over the distant winking lights on the mainland. Thurm and Harry got to laughing over that old family legend about your dad, Harry, winning this property on Orcas Island in a poker game; I always believed it. In any case, it makes a better story than if he had just bought it and divided it among his four children, don't you think? Harry helped himself to a few libations after he put Joan to bed, and he swears up and down that the story is true, and I'm not sure even you know for sure.

A year after that gathering, I'm sorry to tell you that Aunt Sally died. Mom took it badly, and Uncle Dave is still adrift. I don't know if he'll sell the place in Waldport or not. I know you don't like to dwell on clinical information, but it had something to do with her innards, and it was a blessing that she went quickly, the Christian Science practitioner at her side. Mom arrived by plane in time to say goodbye. Mary has been a great comfort to Dave. He may get a place closer to her in Richmond.

Finally, just last year, we had another Tub Thump, this time in Oregon. It was at John and Sue's in Gold Beach. Sue did a hero's job pulling it all together. The cast of characters included most of the Coopers and the Pattons: Bob and Marjorie, Uncle Dave, Mary (Ruth had to work; she drives a bus for the SF Muni), Mom, Bob and Dorothy, Toby and Carrie, Sharon and Selby, George and Marsha, Andy and Mary Jane, etc. I was relieved we didn't have to wear hats like the ones in 1988—remember how they made everyone look like Crazy Guggenheim? And of course, the Voyes were there in force. Mom rented a couple of condos, and Rob and his girls and Anne and her two girls all flew out from Salt Lake, and it was like a three-day slumber party!

John had us all over for a barbecue. He lives back off the coast highway about three miles down a winding narrow road. His house is a big ramshackle place set at the base of a steep hill where a horse roams freely. The property slopes down to a creek and woods. The yard is rough and green, even in summer. Sue has a prolific garden out there that is surrounded with chicken wire to keep out marauding animals and small children. We barbecued on a large wooden deck that John built himself. He got big burlap sacks of oysters which he grilled—they were wonderful. So was the salmon that Andy caught out on the ocean the next day. Mom made the spice cake and your recipe for the chocolate frosting, just like she made for my wedding. You would have loved it all.

Sue and the boys and I went rafting down the Rogue River the next day. We floated lazily most of the time, watching fluffy white clouds above the towering Douglas firs reflected in the cold swift river. Occasionally, there were rapids, and our guide showed us how to maneuver our inflatables through the rapids safely. He told us to look for bears and elk along the riverbank. The boys brought along some water toys that looked like bilge pumps, and they had a fine time squirting each other. We stopped at a sandy bank and had a snack. I found what looked like a bear track near some olallieberry bushes, but one of the boys ran across it before

I could show it to the guide. A jet boat that takes tourists up the river roared past us, and the boys squirted the passengers with their water cannon. It was fun.

I didn't mention yet that I was the sole representative of my own family—Bruce had to work, Liz was volunteering at Marin General Hospital, and Brendan had football camp. I really wish they had come along; they would have enjoyed it. But it was nice for me to have some time for myself and visit with my other relatives that I don't see much of. I so wish you had been there. I still miss you. But I don't think of you as gone. You're just over that hill, where I can't quite see you. I love you. I still have your music box that plays "O Gentle Presence." Please say a prayer for us and for the world. I'm not sure it has really improved since you were here with us.

★★★

1975

The phone rang two times; it was the dead of night. A phone call at that time couldn't be bringing good news, and it wasn't. "Lee, this is Rob," my brother said. "Hi, Rob," I said, wondering why he would be calling at oh-dark-thirty on a Sunday morning.

"Sally's dead. She's been murdered," he said, his voice wavering like a warped record, low and harsh.

"Oh God, oh God." I turned face down on the quilt, the phone jammed between my neck and shoulder. I thought, *Please let this be a nightmare.* I clamped my eyes tight as fists, as if I could prevent the day from awakening, shut out this reality. Rob waited silently on the other end of the phone line.

"Are they sure?" I sputtered, pleading for some hope that the coroner's office that had called Rob had made a misidentification, somebody else had her purse, or . . . "They're sure," he said. The air seemed to thicken and churn. It can't be.

How? Why? This can't be happening. I felt a heavy webbing covering me as if I were a jungle cat trapped in a net. I fought clear of the bedclothes and sat upright on the edge of the bed, my toenails clawing at the cold wood floor. Outside the window, the streetlight fought too, not to be diminished by the brightening dawn.

Rob explained that Sally had been sitting in her car at 2:00 or 3:00 a.m. with prison activist Popeye Jackson as she dropped him off at his flat on

Albion Street after an event in San Francisco. The two of them were shot multiple times by someone, someone unknown. In swift seconds, their lives had drained away.

"Why . . .," I bleated. "We don't know why. Nobody does," Rob said.

I pictured Sally striding through life with purpose, demanding love and respect and receiving it in equal measure. She looked like everyone's image of Alice in Wonderland, long blonde hair and big brown eyes set in a heart-shaped face. Like Alice, she had dropped into an underworld full of strange and dangerous characters. In the days to come, there would be photos of her in the paper that were taken from her driver's license, grinning broadly. Where was the God I thought I knew, the one who couldn't possibly let something like this happen?

I knew that since becoming involved with prison reform and ex-prisoners, Sally had had bullet holes repaired in her car, telling no one but me about the incident but refusing to give details. She said in a vague way that one of her ex-con friends had borrowed the car, laughing off my concern that she had been in danger. She viewed it as if she were John Wayne in a movie, dodging Apache arrows. She knew the people she had begun to be involved with were bred in violence. Sally had taken chances, living as if she would last forever. Until now, none of us who loved her realized just how dangerous her path had become.

I said, "Are Mom and Dad—" Rob interrupted, "They are on their way back from Oregon. I called Bob Veatch, and he drove all the way up there to tell them." I pictured my dad's best friend from his hometown getting the late-night call, getting dressed, and driving thirty-five miles from his home in Klamath Falls through the dark night because there was no phone at the lakeside summer cabin of his childhood friend. I could see Bob clattering over the old porch and beating on the screen door, rehearsing one more time how he would tell Dad that Sally had been murdered.

Bruce was shocked by the news but not numbed enough to weaken him; he took command of coffee, breakfast, dishes, and making the bed. He drove us across the Bay Bridge to my parents' house in Alamo. I was like a mummy, embalmed.

In the car, my respite of composure gave way to sobs. I wished I could cry for weeks, months, but it wouldn't bring Sally back to life. Bruce opened the car windows as if my sound could be sucked out in the open where it would disappear. Finally, he said, "You have to be strong for your family." I scrunched my eyelids and ground my teeth, and in a minute, my noise was gone. I, the star of this drama, was unwell, so an understudy stepped in, someone who looked like me, and acted out my part. But somewhere backstage, the real me was slumped in a corner, still crying.

We rushed along, on cruise control, in between the measured freeway dots and steely instructions: Yield, Merge, Go Back, You Are Going the Wrong Way. We sped through Berkeley, the Caldecott Tunnel, Orinda, and Lafayette. I stared out the windows at the familiar route to my parents' home, where Sally and I had been so healthy and young and our lives were so full of possibility. Even after I went away, to college, to work, to marriage, the house remained the center of our family traditions of Thanksgivings, Christmases, Easters, Mother's Days, Father's Days, and birthdays. It was a big house, and my parents loved having their now grown children's friends over. Dad always took special delight in my brother's friends, all of whom enjoyed making my father laugh. But this would be no day for laughter.

Bruce parked the car under a giant mastodon of a Japanese maple that threw its shade on the semicircular driveway. We walked around to the patio door; nobody used the front door except Jehovah's Witnesses and Girl Scouts selling cookies and other uninviteds. Though it was still early morning, June had already started heating up the day. I looked through the side gate to the pool area and its now-mature landscaping. The small plants that on my wedding day three years ago had been neatly sprigged into the soil like hair transplants had grown luxuriant, hiding the bald patches in between. The shrubs along the fence looked natural and serene, and the trees had grown almost tall enough to hide the telephone wires. The four Sequoia sempervirens were tall and imperious, thriving despite being out of the cool coastal fog that was the redwoods' natural habitat. I walked out and sat for a moment on the diving board, looking at the showy bed of white petunias that had been the backdrop for so many of my wedding photos. "First," I recalled the photographer had said, "let's shoot the mother and father with the bride," as if he was directing a firing squad.

Bruce checked the thermometer that hung suspended in the pool by its own miniature life preserver. The pool was 82, and the day would be over 100 but still cooler than my wedding day when it sizzled.

Inside the house, Sally's typewriter was set up on one of the coffee tables, surrounded by her kindergarteners' report cards. The end of the following week would be the last day of school, and Sally had brought the report cards to Mom and Dad's to work on over the weekend. Apparently, she had been planning to drive from San Francisco to Alamo after the Saturday night party and spend Sunday working on the report cards. She often came here to spend the night, swim, do her laundry, and, lately, talk about her work in the prison reform movement to anyone who would listen. She had left a sign on the typewriter carriage in her neat blackboard capitals: "DO NOT TOUCH! Will clean up in the morning." Of course, no one had dared to touch it. My eyes burned as I thought of the little five-year-old faces who would be told tomorrow that their teacher wouldn't be coming back.

I hugged Rob and Anne and greeted their friends who were already gathered. The shades were down as if to shut out the world, and I walked around, unable to find repose. Grief settled on the family room like a curse. Finally, I yanked on the shade cords, and light blasted in the windows. None of us knew how to behave; no guidelines had been established in our world because nothing like a violent death had ever touched us before. "Let's not act like this is a funeral parlor," I said, suddenly angry.

Mom and Dad finally drove in from Oregon after an eight-hour drive, and we walked outside to the garage to hug them. Dad looked grim, and Mom was red-eyed as they unloaded their car, which ticked and crackled like a furnace. Their dog, Howdy, was oblivious to our grief, just happy to see all of us. I could hear insects singing in the dry grass beyond the fence. Mom went into their bedroom to lie down for a while, and Dad busied himself with sorting the mail that had accumulated during the weeks they had been in Oregon. He answered the phone; reporters were calling. Dad poured himself a cocktail: two jiggers of bourbon, two spoonfuls of sugar, a maraschino cherry, over ice. His jaw slipped off to one side the way it always did as he concentrated on working the spoon as it jittered around in the glass and the sugar swirled into oblivion. Later, Mom poured her own drink of vodka from the freezer and moved purposefully in the kitchen, sponging off countertops that weren't in real need and brushing wisps of her hair back with her forearm. A fan blew hot air around in the family room.

Grandmother arrived and said to Mom, "I remember how you came so quick when Daddy passed," referring to Grandpop. I sat on the couch with Grandmother and listened to her calm theories of death. The fan blew its steady exhale across us.

"I like to think the person is on the other side of a hill," she said as she had always maintained. "You know they are there, but you just can't see them. They are still part of the universe," she said. Grandmother's Christian Science was always about "knowing the truth," something she said when we were sick or injured. All of us wryly told each other to "know the truth" when we slammed a finger in the door or stubbed a toe.

Grandmother had achieved a spiritual level that perhaps can only be discerned when you are older and have seen it all or think you have. I hadn't found my faith yet, but I hoped that I would comprehend the mysteries of religion like she and Gma did someday. Grandmother had taught us a child's prayer: "Father, Mother, God, loving me, guide my little feet up to thee." I did have a teeny bit of trouble with the image of being pulled feet first up to heaven. My playmates as a child recited a different prayer: "Now I lay me down to sleep, I pray the Lord my soul to keep. If I should die before I wake, I pray the Lord my soul to take." I found that prayer unnecessarily morbid; the notion you were signing over your soul to the possibility of death every night was preposterous and what a negative way to end a child's carefree day, you know?

A longtime family friend, Dad's next-door neighbor while growing up in Klamath Falls, opened the sliding glass door and brought in a huge ham studded with pineapple circles and skewered like a porcupine with cherries on toothpicks. She brought several salads and two large cheesecakes in springform pans. "Oh, I'm not going to be any use at all." She wept on Mom's shoulder. She recovered, however, and proceeded to make herself very useful, dishing out salads, cutting the ham, and serving cheesecake with its crunchy nutted crust. One of Sally's boyfriends from high school showed up, pale and shaken.

I sat at the dining table, eating mechanically but not tasting, feeling that any minute Sally would slide open the patio door, with her laundry bag over her shoulder, her long blonde hair swinging, ready for some fun. The house, for a while, almost had a party atmosphere and then became almost peaceful as the afternoon wore on, though new visitors would enter crying and set everyone else off again.

In the early evening, the TV was turned on for the news. The newscasters did feature the crime of the previous night that left two dead on Albion Street. It was big news, I realized bitterly, not because of Sally's death but because Popeye Jackson was a well-known radical speaker and agitator who wanted prison reform. We were as yet unaware of Jackson's role in the tumultuous politics of that time in San Francisco, but all that would unfold in the weeks and months to follow.

A TV crew had apparently arrived on the Albion Street scene as the ambulance attendants were removing the bodies from Sally's car. A small group of neighbors could be seen in the background, their heads bobbing in the whirling red beacon lights from many squad cars.

"Oh God," Mom cried, "they're dragging her out by her feet!" She fled into the bedroom, sobbing. Horror and outrage filled the room. I couldn't believe they would show that on TV; the dead needed to be covered. Like Antigone, I thought it went against the rules of decency and respect. I shut off the TV. None of us could take any more, and the close protective huddle we had maintained all day broke apart as we dispersed into the night.

As I lay awake back in our bed on Green Street in San Francisco, I wondered again what sort of person could walk up to a car and shoot the people sitting in it. Drowsy now, I wondered if dying was like sleep. Outside the tall mullioned windows was the pale opal of the moon, the same moon that brightened the sky over Albion Street the night before, lightening the gray fog covering the city as two bodies leaned together in death, their warm blood dripping into the street. And later in the moonlight, a worker with a hose would have washed their bright blood into the gutters, flowing underneath the city's hard skin through the storm drains that finally emptied into the slate-colored bay.

San Francisco Chronicle

Prison Reformer Dead, Mystery Gunman Kills Two in SF; Execution Slaying in Parked Car

Prison Reformer Wilbert (Popeye) Jackson was shot and killed at point blank range as he sat in a parked car in the Mission District early yesterday.

His woman companion, a 28 year old schoolteacher named Sally Voye, was also killed by a young assailant who leaned in the window of the car after shooting them and pumped more bullets into Jackson's body.

"He appeared to be intent on shooting Popeye," said homicide Inspector Frank Falzon. Falzon and his partner Dave Toschi said the only witness was a 13-year old girl whose name was withheld. She told officers she saw a slim black man between the ages of 18 and 20 fire into the window on the driver's side.

The police said the car was parked in front of 43 Albion Street, where Jackson had been living in a second-floor flat with a woman named Pat Singer. The car engine was cold, indicating the couple had arrived at Jackson's home at least 30 minutes before police arrived.

Police said they did not know the motive for the execution-style slaying of Jackson, a 45-year old ex-convict who founded the United Prisoners Union.

The young witness apparently heard several shots at about 3 a.m. and looked through a stairwell opening in her apartment house in time to see the assailant holding a gun against the already-shattered car window. She told police he ran down Albion toward the Valencia Gardens, a racially-mixed low-income housing project at Valencia and 15th Streets. Immediately after the shooting, the girl was moved to another address for security reasons.

Police found the blood-spattered bodies leaning against each other. Both had been shot in the head and chest, five shell casings from a 9 mm handgun were found at the scene.

Ms. Voye was killed, they speculated, because "since she was there she had to go too."

"We've ruled out robbery," said Toschi. "Both victims had money in their pockets, jewelry on and Ms. Voye's purse with money and other valuables was on the back seat in plain view. I would say this young man was very likely waiting for Popeye to come back home. It seems he knew where Popeye had been and he knew when he was coming back."

Ms. Singer, nine months pregnant with Jackson's child, told police Jackson and Ms. Voye had been to a party, but insisted she did not know where the party was. "I heard the shots," she said. "They woke me up, but I didn't get out of bed or come downstairs."

Ms. Singer said she had been living with Jackson and his three-year-old son from a previous liaison for the past year. She said she holds a staff position in the United Prisoners Union, "doing whatever."

Other members of the union who gathered at the Albion Street flat yesterday said they knew of no threats against Jackson except "the usual ones from the cops, like 'we'll get you yet.'"

Nevertheless, said a man who identified himself only as Sleepy, "[w]e were angry but not surprised. Popeye has had a lot of enemies, one of whom is the police. There are also right wingers and racists."

The union members acknowledged that they have recently been "constructively critical" of certain leftist groups like the Weather Underground and the Symbionese Liberation Army, but said "it would be a meaningless thing for somebody on the left to have done this." They said the prisoners union's only major recent activity was moving its office from 3077 24th street to 1899 Oak Street.

Ms. Voye, they said, was not a member of the union, but had been helping to set up school lectures on prison reform for Jackson and other union members. Police said she lived with a roommate at 190 West K Street in Benicia and taught kindergarten through third grade at Loma Vista Primary School in Vallejo.

She was a graduate of the University of California at Santa Barbara and received her teaching credential from UC Berkeley, according to her father, Joseph Voye of Alamo. Voye said his daughter had not talked to him about Jackson, but had "mentioned at one time that she was sympathetic" to the prison reform group. She was active in a teacher's union, he said, but to his knowledge was not interested in any other political activities.

Friends from her Santa Barbara days, where she became president of Pi Beta Phi sorority, agreed she hadn't been a particularly political person. But they said she developed a strong sensitivity about social injustices since graduating. "She was sort of a not-political idealist, a good person—the kind more of us should be like," said an ex-roommate and good friend who asked not to be identified.

Her female friends said that she—like all of them—had changed their social outlooks considerably since their idyllic sorority days in Santa Barbara. Having been enclosed in first Alamo and then Santa Barbara, "Sally really didn't know about a lot of things that are part of urban life," noted a college friend, a social worker who now lives in Albany and kept in reasonably close touch with Sally over the years.

Jackson spent 19 years in prison for robbery and burglary convictions before his parole four years ago. Shortly after his release, he was elected to the board of directors of the California Prisoners Union, according to John Irwin, who still serves on the California Prisoners Union board.

But Jackson left that group and formed the United Prisoners Union about two years ago, Irwin said. Both groups, who claim to represent convicts and ex-convicts, have strongly criticized the state and federal penal systems and advocated various kinds of changes.

"We have been somewhat at odds with Popeye," Irwin acknowledged. "We have kept our distance for the last few years for a variety of reasons. Popeye is a person who I would guess would have dozens and dozens of enemies, but I have been so far away from his personal life for so many years I would have no idea who they are."

Irwin said the two unions are not rival groups, since "we were able to cooperate on a lot of public issues. We had common interests, but at the same time we had nothing to do with each other."

Jackson was arrested in August of 1973 on charges of heroin and marijuana possession, but claimed police planted the drugs in his car. He was acquitted after a jury trial the following November. In April of last year, he was again arrested on a misdemeanor charge of "interfering with a police officer in the performance of his duty."

After the Los Angeles gunbattle of May 17, 1974 in which six members of the Symbionese Liberation Army were killed, Jackson appeared at "memorial rallies" for the six and denounced the shooting as a "police massacre."

★ ★ ★

The following day, the *San Francisco Chronicle* reported that investigators had few clues yesterday to the shooter of Popeye and Sally. Apparently, the police investigation was being hindered by "guarded answers and a generally hostile atmosphere" on the part of Jackson's friends and associates.

The report stated that Inspector David Toschi of the police homicide detail said Jackson, forty-five, was shot four times in the shoulder, chest, and head and that Ms. Voye, a Vallejo schoolteacher, was shot five times in the back and head.

Our family mourned. Who could have done such a thing? I want to know *why*. Each day, the newspapers screamed lurid headlines and brought more shock and outrage with new developments in the investigation. My family huddled together in the heat and tried to make sense of it all. And there was no shortage of far-out groups to either take credit for the assassinations or blame another group for them.

★★★

An article in the *San Francisco Examiner* on Wednesday, June 11, screamed that "Popeye was a pig." A communique from the New World Liberation Front had said that they believed that Jackson was a revolutionary vanguard not only in appearance but also in action, serving as an example to all the oppressed people, but had become an "elitist pig," serving his own personal needs and misleading the people's forces. The communique further stated that "Popeye Jackson lacked principle, ideology and knowingly worked to serve the interests of the pigs and ruling class which kept the oppressed people from building a strong, unified and secure base."

★ ★ ★

I needed to get back to work; idleness had become stifling. Back in our San Francisco flat on Green Street, I spent a lot of time in bed, trying to sleep, or on the phone with my family. Bruce had gone back to work midweek and encouraged me to do the same instead of wandering around the flat like a zombie.

Daybreak brought the garbage trucks, snarling and growling like jackals underneath my window. I dressed, descended from our flat, and walked down to Union Street where I caught the 45 bus for the financial district.

I had worked at a financial consulting firm for three years. I had called in Monday to our office manager to say I wouldn't be in for a couple of days because my sister had been killed. When he pressed for details, I told him to look on the front page of the *Chronicle*. He must have read the paper already, saying, "That's your sister?" I couldn't face the office. I needed to be around family and close friends. He said something about a funeral, and I lied that it would be at the end of the week.

There would be no funeral; my parents hated funerals. What my dad really meant was that he never wanted to see everybody crying; it was for him a messy display of emotion. When Gma died several years before, the mortuary Down There handled all of it, and none of us grandchildren were even invited, it being "too far to travel" according to Mom and Dad, and it was on a weekday when we all were working. I would have preferred some proof that she was really gone, but open casket funerals and lines of mourners and gravesite interment just weren't our family's style. The ashes were scattered, and that was the end of it.

And if there was no funeral for Sally, maybe I could pretend it didn't happen. I hated that Sally's ashes would be scooped out of the ovens and scattered by deckhands off some boat under contract with the Neptune Society whenever it was convenient. Mom, Dad, and I drove one afternoon to the Golden Gate Bridge, and Mom dropped a wreath of daisies and roses into the water that swirled around the bridge's tower base and sucked it slowly on an ebb tide, out to sea. No service, no clergy, no black dresses, no hearses, no tears. No spadefuls of dirt raining down on a casket. Person erased, simple, clean, and painless.

Except I found out the hard way that pain gets trapped inside and builds like steam inside a boiler. Grief needs to be exorcised, I would conclude after the events of Sally's death brought me to a full understanding of how I needed to immerse myself in mourning to come out the other side. Letting go is a natural progression. I needed to go through the shock, disbelief, rage, and then slow realization that I wouldn't be the same again for a long time. I yearned for a body to say farewell to.

But that week, I didn't know that yet. I was not in control of events. I was not aware that suppressing grief would be a big mistake. I feared being bad company, but I went back to work anyway two days after Sally's murder and tried to show some grace.

I had started out working for stockbrokers after college, and finally after a couple of lateral moves, I ended up in the field of municipal finance. I knew little about muni bonds at the beginning, but I trained on the job and found out that few public officials know enough about the topic, so they want to hire someone to deal with it. Our firm was hired by cities, counties, and special districts to take care of the business of the sale of bonds to build a municipal project, such as a library, civic center, or water treatment plant.

I spent the next few days working furiously on a schedule for some bonds destined to finance a sewage treatment plant. My high school experience reporting to the local newspaper about the sewer district came in handy. I knew the lingo: *outfall, sewerage, tertiary treatment* . . . As the computer spewed a printout of the schedule, I looked out the window at the cold blue bay and wondered why the concept of present value scares people. Compound interest and discount rates also make people snaky. I think in my next life I'll be a landscaper or an archaeologist.

When I was in the fifth grade, I won a contest that the teacher, Mrs. Garner, presented to the class: to identify every fairy-tale character pictured together on a big color poster. There was Alice in Wonderland, Hansel and Gretel, Humpty Dumpty, Paul Bunyan, Cinderella, and more, all in one big picture. My prize for correctly naming the most characters was a book, but not of fairy tales. It was a book about the ancient city of Troy in the Middle East and how its ruins had been discovered in the 1920s by a German archaeologist named Heinrich Schliemann. From then on, I was in love with the idea of being an archaeologist, discovering lost cities, lost tribes, and implements with clues as to how ancient people lived. I longed to dust bones with a tiny brush and divine the secrets of civilization, but in the end, I followed a more practical career path, one that would not require digging or tsetse flies or scorpions or carbon-dating old artifacts.

I ripped the paper out of the computer and trimmed off the sprocket holes. I had enjoyed my work for the past few years, and I looked forward to nesting, buying a house out of the city, and having kids. Now I felt a chill toward the city. Since Sally had died here, San Francisco seemed to me fuller of threat than ever, a kind of evil sandbox for grown-ups. Children wouldn't be safe if adults weren't either.

My coworkers were kind enough about Sally's death. Most of them murmured something and slunk away with downcast eyes. I received them with all the grace I could summon, which probably wasn't much. A few of them actually said too much. "Aren't ya bummed out?" bounced a post-teen-aged secretary who was known to smoke pot in her car on her lunch hour. *Duh*, I thought silently. "Sorry about the thing with Sally," said another. *The thing* . . .

The *San Francisco Chronicle* lay on the table in the coffee room, each day its front page reporting some new development in the murders, and my coworkers avoided going into the coffee room when I was in there . A couple of my coworkers said nothing at all, as if they were afraid I might be reminded. As if I could forget. Our receptionist, Leon, said he was sorry for my loss. When he first came to our employ, he said he lived in Sausalito, and I said, "Do you take the ferry home?" to which he replied, "Honey, I've taken so many fairies home." He said he was from a family of nine children, and according to him, "Ah'm the only one who's nawmul."

Then there was Sean. The whole time we worked together, Sean had said too much about everything. He blabbed all day on the phone, and he nattered at staff meetings while others tried not to nod off. My first day back at the office he invited me to join him on the rooftop deck to eat our sandwiches. This was unusual; we weren't exactly buddies. We sat on the chairs on the wooden decking that we employees had installed on the rooftop one Saturday. Our building dated from the thirties, and unlike the all new high-rises, it had windows that you could actually open for air. Our suite was on the top floor, so we also had access to the roof, and our principals got permission from the building owners to improve the rooftop for employees' use.

Today, the sun was warm; the morning fog had burned off. I sat with my eyes closed for a while; it was the first time I'd been in the sun for several days. I could see the shimmering sapphire bay with Mt. Tamalpais off in the distance and the Golden Gate Bridge. We sat for a time without talking until, true to form, Sean broke the silence. He just couldn't let it be; silence was something for him that just cried out to be filled. Usually, by the end of a workday, Sean's voice would be hoarse.

"My father shot himself," confided Sean, chomping on his sandwich. I never knew this. I stammered that I was sorry; my sourdough bread turned sandy in my mouth. "Many, many years ago," he said with a little wave as if he'd come to grips with it. I tried to picture his father, probably heavy bearded and loquacious like his son. Sean continued to chatter about his dead father. "Irish," he said, as if that explained it.

"I've always wondered how it sounds, bullets going into a skull . . .," Sean droned on as I looked over the parapet, thirty stories above the tiny toy cars and people the size of ants below. I felt dizzy. Sean and I should have had a common bond with our experience with violent death, but . . . no. I wished a huge King Kong would reach out his hairy paws and rescue me from the rooftop and carry me back to a peaceful jungle and away from Sean, away from all the craziness. I stood and looked again over the edge. Lunch was over. I floated down the stairs into the office where I was safe from talk of bullets and skulls.

The next day, another bewildering headline in the *Chronicle* said, "Radicals Now Say They Didn't Kill 'Popeye.'"

"A new message—also claiming to be from the New World Liberation Front—denied yesterday that the radical group was responsible for the murder of Wilbert 'Popeye' Jackson of the United Prisoners Union. Yesterday's message contradicted a message left in a South-of-Market phone booth Tuesday, purportedly signed by the New World Liberation Front and claiming credit for the shootings. However, the newest message congratulated Jackson's murder, saying: 'We commend him/them for his/ their action in the interests of the oppressed people toward creating a snitch free base . . .' ('Snitch' is underworld slang for a police informer.) But yesterday's message criticized Jackson's killer for 'the murder of Sally Voye, who appeared to be innocent . . .'

"Among other things, the police are checking out an anonymous telephone call received by them Tuesday which claimed that the Aryan Brotherhood, a white racist gang at San Quentin Prison, paid a killer $1,000 to murder Jackson, a black man.

"Jackson's family and Pat Singer, the woman with whom he lived and the mother of the slain man's unborn child, held a press conference at Glide Memorial Church in San Francisco yesterday afternoon. The family and Ms. Singer denied recently-published charges that the Prisoners Union organizer was an opportunist, a police informer, or a man of personal wealth . . ."

On Thursday, the *Examiner* reported that Wilbert "Popeye" Jackson, the convict-rights leader gunned to death early Sunday, had been the target of an earlier assassination attempt. I knew, Sally had told me this. Apparently, Jackson; Pat Singer, the woman who is nine months pregnant with his child; and two other persons were riding in a car (Sally's car) in the Mission District. At least one shot was fired at the car, striking it on the roof. No one in the car was injured. Although police theorized that Jackson was the obvious target, Toschi cautioned yesterday to not overlook Sally, stating that she "belonged to Jackson's United Prisoners Union but she had not played an extremely active role in it."

My family couldn't reconcile any of this. Radicals and terrorists were lined up to weigh in on the crime and assign blame. A rally in Benicia that night was held to remember Sally, but none of us attended.

★ ★ ★

On Saturday, even before I got out of the car, I could smell the roses blooming in a rainbow of colors in the side yard of Sally's house in Benicia. I parked my car in front, and Mom and I walked into the rose garden. We were waiting for Grandmother and Anne to catch up; Grandmother always drove her Buick in the slow lane. We needed two cars to clear out Sally's belongings.

Mom and I wandered through the roses like bees, lost in the spicy fragrance. Each bush had been pruned to grow upright, tall as a person, loaded with blossoms. Each had its own color and perfume. Could it only be one month since Sally brought us all corsages she made from these roses?

"Remember how Sally always used to refuse to recognize any flower except daisies and roses?" Mom asked me as she snapped off a perfect white tea rose and held it to her nose. I smiled at the memory of how Mom spent hours poring over the *Sunset Western Garden Book*, designing her garden, planting, and maintaining the large flower garden in Alamo. When she talked of their botanical names such as *ranunculus, calendulas, myoporum, rhaphiolepsis*, and the like, Sally dismissed them all with "Face it, Mom, it's all just daisies and roses." I thought of the wreath, white daisies, and roses that Mom tossed off the bridge just a week ago.

One month ago was Mother's Day at Grandmother's in Menlo Park, the last time I would see Sally. She brought corsages she made from the roses in this garden for all of us: Mom, Aunt Sally, Grandmother, Anne, and me. She sprigged the roses with forget-me-nots that also grew here in the side yard against the fence. She had twisted green florist's tape around the stems and tied them with white satin ribbons and packed them into a long coffin-like box lined with tissue paper, very professional. She brought long stick pins with pearl heads to pin them on with. "How lovely these corsages are, prettier than anything from the florists," said Grandmother as Sally worked the pin into the lapel of Grandmother's blouse.

After our lunch, Sally had complained of cramps, so she went back into Grandmother's bedroom to lie down. Dad, Uncle Dave, Bruce, and Grandmother watched baseball on TV, and Aunt Sally and Mom did the dishes. I went into the bedroom to check on Sally. She lay on her back, her feet off to the side of Grandmother's quilt, a multicolored double wedding ring made by Grandmother's mother, Elizabeth Jordan. Elizabeth had quilted a Celtic knot pattern in the centers of the rings, a strong reminder of the family forebears.

Sally looked peaceful lying there, but she was pale, and there was a weariness, a kind of weight to her voice. "I'd like to see you more," she said, and it was true that now that I was married and lived on Green Street in San Francisco and she had moved to Benicia, we hadn't gotten together much in the last couple of years, except for holidays like today. I said I'd like that too and sat down in the rocker next to the old Emerson radio console on which Grandmother listened to Christian Science lectures and read her Bible daily.

"Do you think you'll have kids?" she asked me, staring at the ceiling. Outside, long purple wisteria blossoms peeked into the windows, their fragrance drifting in the open screens like a deep tidal current, the bees humming at their work.

I said, "Yeah, sure, in a couple of years after we have our own nest." In fact, after saving for almost four years, we were close to having enough for a down payment and would purchase our first house in Marin County at the end of the following year.

"I've pretty much given up on the idea of ever getting married and having kids," Sally said, shifting her legs on the bed. I was stunned. Of anyone I could think of, she would be a great mother. And Sally always had boyfriends galore, and her professional life as a teacher was dedicated to kids, and she was very good with them. My mind flashed back to high school and college when she always dated the guys who were the coolest— the basketball players, fraternity guys, cheerleaders, and the class president. We ripened together, but she always seemed to get picked. Many times in our teens, I was stiff with jealousy as she waltzed off to the parties and dances, sometimes with boys from *my* grade, while I sat home with my little brother and sister and popcorn.

Sally never actually stole a boyfriend from me, but who knew how many boys were diverted by her good blonde looks, her self-confidence, her high-spiritedness? Next to her I felt invisible, geeky, and way too tall and skinny. She had a nice round nose; I had a beak. She had smooth blonde hair; mine was frizzy and rat brown. Next to her, I felt homely as a mud fence. I had no choice but to cultivate a wacky, self-deprecating persona in order to be noticed, and it actually worked. I was voted Funniest my senior year in high school. I still wonder how others in that listing—Most Likely to Succeed, Best Personality, Smartest—lived up to their billing? I know I'm not funny anymore. Is Bruce A. successful?

I was suddenly aware that for the first time, Sally may actually have been a tiny bit envious of me. I had a husband and a chance for children and a home. Was that too bourgeoisie, or was that what she wanted? I knew she'd recently broken up with Don, someone she considered marrying, but he was only separated and had decided to reconcile with his wife. She was still hurting over that. Before that was a guy who adored her but was out of the question because he was a cop. And another man, Tom, still called her, but she said she just couldn't get too excited about someone whose dinner invitations were "Why don't you stay for dinner, I've got some burger that's just about to go bad."

She hadn't met the man who was perfect for her. But to give up on children, at age twenty-eight, just because you're currently single? Something was wrong, but I couldn't tell what. "Why do you say that?" was all I could manage to say. Maybe the cramps were clouding her vision of her future.

"It's just not going to happen," she declared with conviction, and it was as if she knew she only had a few weeks to live. Then after a silence, she said something that was just as disturbing.

"I know where Patty Hearst is." When I asked where, she said she couldn't say.

"Can't you save her?" I blurted. She said enigmatically, "Patty doesn't need to be saved."

Patty Hearst had been kidnapped in Berkeley the year before, and it would be another half a year before she was found. Little did I know of

Sally's peripheral connection to that whole sordid cops and robbers drama. Finally, Sally sat up on the edge of the bed and yawned. From the kitchen, Grandmother sang, "Ice cream!" and we walked back into the living room as the SF Giants baseball crowd on TV groaned at a strikeout.

★ ★ ★

At last, Grandmother and Anne drove up in front of Sally's Benicia house. It was a tired Victorian, its fireproof shingling curling and shrinking in the sun like fried bacon. Grandmother and Anne took a quick tour of the roses, but Mom said we had work to do. Anne sniffed at a blood-red rose and then walked onto the swaybacked porch to read a plaque that was tacked to the sandpapery shingles near the front door. She read it aloud, "Historical Landmark, Hobson House, Built 1882."

Sally had been enthused about moving last year from Berkeley into the big old house, a sentinel from another era. Also, Benicia was a closer drive than Berkeley to the school where she taught in Vallejo. Benicia had many historical buildings; it was one of California's earliest towns. Sally's house faced a square green park just a few blocks from the old State Capitol building that served as California's state capital in 1853 and 1854.

Finally, we forced ourselves to go inside the house. We found Sally's two roommates cheerlessly packing boxes. Rather than find another roommate to share the rent here, they had found an apartment for two nearby. The big old place felt gloomy; I wouldn't have wanted to stay either.

We walked down a narrow hallway grooved with wainscoting and lined with a long gray runner. The rug led us past the double parlors and the staircase to the kitchen and dining room where, I observed when I visited last winter, the three roommates spent most of their time; it was the warmest place in the house. Sally said complaints to the landlord produced few results. The roof leaked, the front porch was rotten, there were mice, but her main concern was the heat or the lack of it. The one ancient gas heater was located in the living room, three chairs still arranged in a semicircle a few inches from the heater. Each roommate had her own portable electric heater in her upstairs bedroom. The parlors, the attic, the basement, and the service porch had all mostly lain fallow and unused, waiting for a thaw.

I walked into the cool front parlor where Sally's grand piano was. Sunlight filtered through the layers of dust coating the tall windows. I sat on the bench and plinked out a small melody I had learned years ago from Mrs.

Close, from whom Sally and I took piano lessons. Mrs. Close was ample like risen dough, and she always smelled of oranges. At the end of that year when she was to move away, she gave us each a card with pictures of Mozart and Chopin surrounded by gold stars. Our new piano teacher looked like Ichabod Crane and always set the metronome ticking on top of the piano. I couldn't bear that sound; it interfered with my heartbeat somehow, and I dropped out of piano lessons. Sally continued. She had inherited the gene with musical talent from Dad and Gma's side of the family. Gma said Sally had "perfect pitch" as apparently, she could sing a note on demand, middle C, for example, or when she heard a note, she could tell if it was A or C or G-flat. She also taught herself to play the guitar.

I leafed through the sheet music on the stand atop the piano. She had volumes of show tunes, folk songs, some pop, and a large stack of children's songs that she must have sung for her kindergarteners. A bud vase on top of the piano held a single dead rose, its head bent over as if in prayer. Sally's cat, Muhammad X, rubbed against my leg and silently showed his teeth. I loaded all the sheet music into a wooden Boss lettuce box. I walked back into the kitchen where Anne was helping Diane, one of the roommates, separate out Sally's pans and utensils.

I climbed the stairs and walked down the second-story hallway, its flowered wallpaper yellowed and water stained. Mom and Grandmother were in Sally's room at the end of the hall. Centering the room was Sally's bed, unmade, its blue and white quilt trailing to the floor on one side. On the bottom sheet in the dead center of the bed was a single spot of blood. It caught my breath, and I had to turn aside. The spot was now burned into my corneas; it was in my throat, a spot so sensitive that it hurt without being touched. The spot, innocent as ketchup on an apron, filled me with such horror that I had to grind my teeth to keep from shuddering. Behind me, Mom and Grandmother were assembling cardboard boxes. I wanted to warn them: Don't look at the blood—it will pierce your heart. But I stood there, struck dumb. I saw the blood of life's renewal, the cycle of life that Sally had forever renounced, the blood that flows out of all women of childbearing age, connecting us to the future.

Grandmother elbowed me aside and briskly stripped the sheets and put them in a black plastic bag designated for garbage. She had two other bags that were assigned for keeping or for the thrift shop. I saw that Mom had seen the blood spot; she bit her lip and looked away. Grandmother knew just what to do; she had outlived her husband and siblings and many of her friends. She attacked the task with such fervor that I thought for a moment she was going to whistle a tune. I watched her opening Sally's bureau drawers and dumping the contents onto the bare mattress. "Can any of you wear this?" she would say; thus, we divided the useful from the rag bag. I wanted some of Sally's clothes, even though Sally was a size smaller—I just wanted something as a talisman.

Anne came in, finished with the kitchen things, and began taking the clothes out of Sally's closet. She held up the old, chewed-looking muskrat coat that Sally had bought at a thrift shop and worn so proudly with blue jeans. Neither Anne nor I could bear to take it, so it was destined to return to its origins, another thrift shop.

I opened Sally's jewelry box. On top of assorted costume jewelry and wooden beads, along with a number of earrings for pierced ears, I found the two turquoise necklaces that Sally wore so often they were practically her trademark. She had bought them during a summer trip to Arizona. I wondered why she hadn't worn them that Saturday night. Did she deliberately dress down so as not to outshine her new acquaintances, flaunt her privilege? I put both necklaces on.

"I want these," I said, as much a statement of fact and a declaration of possession. On the way home later, I would feel selfish for taking both; why hadn't I given Anne one of them? But Sally wore them together; they were a unit, and I couldn't bear the thought of separating them. Besides, Anne had pierced ears. She could have all the earrings, including some really pretty turquoise ones. I, not being into pain, never had my ears pierced. Or any tattoos. I'm wimpy that way.

Our family was a triad of units: Dad and Mom, a couple, unassailable; then Sally and I, a twosome a year apart in age and separated by five and six years from Rob and Anne, the third unit. Now my unit was blown apart; I was alone, the fifth wheel. I had lost a confidant, a sparring partner, a close rival; no one would be pounding at my heels ever again with better grades, better hair, more boyfriends, worthier goals. I claimed those necklaces for small comfort.

We took a break in the park across the street, eating Grandmother's egg salad sandwiches and drinking Dr. Peppers from the can. We sat under a weeping willow, its arching branches clipped off clean underneath, I guessed by deer, straight across like a Dutch boy haircut. At the other side of the park, I could see a white lattice gazebo where a memorial service for Sally had been organized by her roommates just a few evenings before. I walked over there; a stone pillar was marked Dedicated to Eight Brave Men Who Gave Their Lives in the World War. After that war, no one could imagine that there would be another world war just two decades later. I passed young mothers pushing their small offspring on a swing set that was designed like a huge clown, the swings suspended from its outstretched arms. Three boys ran past, snapping toy pistols at each other. One chanted,

"Bang, bang, you're dead,
Fifty bullets in your head,
Brush your teeth, go to bed,
In the morning you'll be dead."

I stood before the gazebo. I hadn't attended the memorial service for no reason explainable to anyone, except that I was afraid that my sadness would engulf me, swallow me into darkness, and I would lose control. Thus, I began a pattern of avoidance, a refusal to face my emotional self, the self that receded over the following years, shriveled, and faded. That part of me entered a hidden room, my rational self unaware that the effects of the tragedy were great or perhaps denying their importance. I was on a path of isolation from my own emotional self.

After our lunch break, we returned to Sally's room, where we moved faster and made quicker decisions to speed up the grim work and get out of there. The closet was now bare, the walls stripped of artwork, the cord wound around the portable heater, ready for storage. Her toothbrush and toiletries were dumped. I was still slogging through Sally's desk, assailed by the messages given off by the radical literature. On her bedside table was a book whose cover showed a pistol pointing out, right at my heart. She had *Soul on Ice*, and another was *Steal This Book*. I scooped up paperbacks and pamphlets, literature about prison reform and education, books by black activists Angela Davis and Eldridge Cleaver, and books on women's concerns by Germaine Greer and Betty Friedan. I threw them all in the bag destined for the used bookstore.

I was mechanical, battery operated, throwing clothes, blankets, underwear, and socks, no longer careful, knowing it really didn't matter. I put a pair of her sandals in my bag to take home, the imprint of her feet molded into them, knowing my own footprints would not mesh. It is said that if you walk in another's shoes, you can understand them; would I be able to understand Sally? I remembered how she would flounce around shoe departments, demanding just the right shoes to fit her special feet. "I have these high insteps," she would explain to the shoe man. She would run her finger up over the high arch that made her special somehow. She'd try dozens of shoes, seldom any of them quite right for her vaunted insteps, making it clear that the shoes that I had selected for myself were all right for mere mortals, but not for her, of the really special feet.

I boxed up the final details of our shared past: Jean Nate cologne and Pikake perfume from the trip Grandmother took with us to Hawaii, horse show ribbons from Shady Lawn Farm, a picture of Gma from under the bureau glass, and a black-and-white photo of Mom and Dad on their wedding day in 1943. None of these gave me a clue as to why she turned out the way she was or why I was me. I opened her top drawer to find stacks and stacks of birth control pills—she had enough to prevent generations of children from being born. Did she think she would live forever? I set my jaw and gathered up all the round plastic holders with their numbered windows and threw all those unborn descendants into the bag designated for the trash.

We took the last of the boxes downstairs, leaving the few pieces of furniture and the piano that Mom had arranged to have picked up and put in storage. I went back up, and the room felt all hollow as I ran a dust mop around the dark parquet floor. I opened the window that let in a bronzy ochre light from the diminishing day. I stuck the dust mop out the window and shook it, watching the dust, her dust, swirl, glittering, down over the roses in the late pale sun.

★ ★ ★

Saturday's *Chronicle* announced that a message "purportedly from the long-dormant Symbionese Liberation Army [SLA] deploring the slaying of prison reform activist Wilbert (Popeye) Jackson, was released yesterday by Berkeley radio station KPFA."

Station spokesmen said they believe the document, dated June 12, is "probably genuine" from its "method of delivery," appearance, and political rhetoric. They would not specify when the statement was received or how it was delivered. FBI agent in charge Charles Bates was somewhat more skeptical after seeing the document. "There is no way to tell whether it is genuine or not," Bates said.

The terrorist SLA, which kidnapped and then converted newspaper heiress Patricia Hearst to its revolutionary philosophy, was last heard from June 7, 1974, in a taped message from Ms. Hearst and fellow fugitives William and Emily Harris. They separately mourned their six comrades who died in a gun battle with police in Los Angeles. The three are believed to be the only surviving members of the so-called army.

"We have long considered Jackson to be a friend and comrade," the SLA communication said. "We supported his work in the prison movement and his outspoken stance in supporting guerrilla fighters. Popeye Jackson was constantly under harassment from the pigs because of his uncompromising position of the armed struggle and the rights of the convicted class." The message suggested that Ms. Voye was "executed for no reason other than being an innocent bystander."

Jackson, who spent 19 years in prison . . .

★ ★ ★

"Jackson, who spent nineteen years in prison . . . blah blah blah." I crumpled up the paper and threw it on the floor. "What is this shit? Investigators are saying don't overlook Sally as an intended target. Every wacko underground group has issued their 'communique,' except maybe the Ku Klux Klan . . . And who the hell actually uses the word *purportedly*? It's like slain—it's 'newspaperese.' This is ridiculous!" I ranted.

Bruce was reading the sports page and wisely made no comment.

The newspaper articles continued; the story still had power. By June 20, another headline in the *Chronicle* said, "Another View of the Popeye Killing." The article said, "Yet another radical group aired its views yesterday on the June 8 killing of prison reformer Wilbert (Popeye) Jackson. A message purportedly smuggled out of San Quentin Prison by the Black Guerrilla Family, a prison organization of militant blacks, saying the killing of Jackson and a friend, Sally Voye, was the work of the pigs."

The message read further, "We did not in any way or form consent to the action that was initiated against Popeye Jackson and Sally Voye. We feel that the murder of (the two) was the work of the pigs. The charges lodged against Popeye, we feel, are void of foundation . . ." It went on to say, "We are not convinced, due to our association and personal knowledge during the stages of incarceration, that Popeye was a snitch."

The article further said that Tribal Thumb was still under investigation in connection with the killings and that their alleged leader, Earl Satcher, was arrested on a parole violation and is being held in the Marin County jail. Later, I would read that the Tribal Thumb name is derived from the commune's "tribal" organization and from the fact that the human hand is useless without the thumb.

It turned out that many of the radical events of the mid-1970s in San Francisco were interrelated, and Patty Hearst's name was often in the conversation. An even earlier event turned out to be the first terrorist murder in radical Bay Area politics: the November 1973 murder of the Oakland superintendent of schools, Marcus Foster. The SLA said it ordered Foster's execution with cyanide bullets because he was trying to put "political police" on school campuses.

The SLA was an "army" of eight or ten losers and misfits who wanted to, what, liberate all symbions? They were led by an ex-con named Donald DeFreeze, who dubbed himself "Cinque." In early 1974, they decided it would be a brilliant idea to kidnap Patricia Hearst of the Hearst family that owned the *San Francisco Examiner*.

So they did. In mid-1974, after Patricia Hearst's kidnapping, the SLA demanded that her father, Randolph Hearst, pay $2 million and then upped it to $4 million in ransom, to be paid out in a free food giveaway program to the Bay Area needy. Popeye Jackson was one of the coalition of activists who had offered to oversee the proposed program, named People in Need (PIN). Popeye had street cred and had developed a rapport with Patty's father. A critical element of the SLA demand was for funds to defend Russell Little and Joseph Remiro on the Marcus Foster murder charges. The two were in custody at San Quentin Prison and were complaining that they were being denied visitors and exercise rights.

Popeye was an influential member of the coalition of groups organizing the food giveaways at a dozen distribution points around the Bay Area. Boxes of food did go to the needy, but in far less quantities than were envisioned. Many of the volunteers and counterculture revolutionaries who waded into the project were incompetent or had their own agenda, such as charging inflated prices for food or its delivery. Some individuals resold the PIN food and pocketed the money. A distribution site in Oakland had been particularly chaotic and disorganized, and riots and injuries had occurred. One volunteer who actually brought order to the San Francisco headquarters of the program was a bookkeeper and general dogsbody named Sara Jane Moore.

The People in Need food giveaway program funded by the Hearsts only lasted a few months, according to the book of Patty's fiancé, Steven Weed, *My Search for Patty Hearst*. Despite the "ransom" that the Hearsts paid, it did not result in Patty's release. In a written communique from the SLA, Patty, still in hiding, called the PIN giveaway a "sham" and said that rather than being released, she was choosing to "stay and fight."

After PIN wound down, Weed made note of the injuries, the jail sentences, the lawsuits, the half-million-dollar "overage" that was to become the Hearsts' responsibility, and the letters from people requesting that their earlier donations to PIN be returned. He also noted that Sara Jane Moore's story was part of the drama and she may have been an informant herself. In September of 1975, "the movement of frustration and disorientation that for Sara had begun with PIN reached the end of its course as she stood in a crowd outside San Francisco's St. Francis Hotel and fired her revolver at President Ford."

Sara Jane Moore would serve thirty-two years in prison for the unsuccessful assassination attempt on President Gerald Ford.

★ ★ ★

A couple of weeks after Sally was killed, I developed hives—raised red welts blossomed on my arms, legs, and torso, preventing any sleeping, not that I had been sleeping much anyway. All night I could feel the maddening itch; it was torture. I wore loose clothing so as to not irritate the itching further, but even that did not help. Bruce smoothed calamine lotion onto my raging skin every few hours. Even with a gentle touch, it was like being pulled naked over gravel. "Sally was just trying to help," I moaned, face down on the bed, inert, the sheets stained with the pink calamine. I was wearing my grief right on my skin.

That second Saturday after Sally's death was Father's Day. We again drove over to the East Bay to see my parents. "Happy Father's Day, Dad," I said, handing him a present. He was sitting in his usual place, the corner of one of the built-in banquettes, facing the TV, though the TV wasn't on. It was not yet noon, but a glass of bourbon was already parked on the windowsill beside the seat.

Dad tore off the wrapping paper and dropped it on the floor. He held it up wordlessly for Mom to see. It was a set of horns, longhorn cattle horns. "I thought you could use it for a coat rack or something or maybe at the cabin . . .," I stammered, embarrassed, cursing myself for being such an eejit. This was beyond stupidity; dads were impossible to buy gifts for, but this one really missed the mark.

"Yeah," muttered Dad, turning away quickly before a tear splashed onto his shirt front. I turned too, thinking it was best for him to regain his composure. Dad hated crying. I ground my teeth and escaped into the kitchen. Sally's high school graduation portrait was propped up on the piano across the room. "She had stars in her eyes," Dad had said, referring to her various crusades for social justice. Years later, I would revisit the memory and wish I had sat close with him, hugged him, and allowed the tears to soak both our shirts. There would only be a few more Father's Days for me and my dad.

On the piano, I found Sally's eighth-grade yearbook, *The Mighty Oak*, from Oak Knoll School. It had been in the bedroom we shared upstairs. I found her pictures in the activities section: with her white letter sweater, the school letters OK on the pocket; as a student council officer, squinting into the sun; as an upper-grade ice cream seller (a real honor), her legs crossed demurely; and as a ballroom monitor. She was one of seven cheerleaders, each standing with arms wide, with one leg bent up underneath a long skirt, looking like snowy egrets.

I read the autographs in the yearbook with all their misspellings:

"Sally: you sure are CUTE. Please stay that way. You will have all the boys next year. Wish I could get my hair the way you have yours. Had fun with you this year. I hope your house doesn't sell so you can stay here! Love, Jean. P.S. come swimming any time!"

"To Sally: I think your one of the nicest girls at Oak Knoll. I'm sure you'll make a big hit when you go to high school. You sure have a good personality besides being cute. You really deserved all those awards at the assembly. You are tops as a pom pom girl. Sincerely, Ernie."

"Sally: to a real cute girl who can be a stinker (so can I.) Good luck always - real sorry to see you move away. Good luck forever, Barry M."

"Sally: You've been a reall good classmate, and I hop you have fun at your queer new high school, get good grades. I wish I was taller, but that doesn't seem to possible. That's one reason I don't like to be short. Good luck, Eddie." I think poor Eddie won't win a spelling bee, nor will he play pro basketball.

"Sally: I love you. Sincerely, Cheryl H."

Sally's self-assurance took off during those junior high years at Oak Knoll. She became outspoken, she was popular, and boys vied for her attention. Some of her friendships were on and off because she told the truth, whether her friends wanted to hear it or not. I was more protective of friendships, I was more insecure, I probably told people what they wanted to hear. I wanted to be loved. Above all, Sally wanted to be right.

Two years after the murders, a suspect was identified: Richard Alan London, who had been arrested for an unrelated crime less than a month after the killings and was in jail. The *San Francisco Chronicle* reported, "In San Francisco on June 8, 1975, a notorious homicide was committed in which one 'Popeye' Jackson and a female companion, Sally Voye, were slain by gunfire. An eyewitness described the crime's perpetrator as a black male with a hairstyle that looked like a short Afro. Less than a month after the murders, Richard Alan London was arrested in Napa County on a warrant from Santa Clara County, on charges of robbery of a Mountain View coin shop. While in custody, London had bragged to a cellmate that he was a real hitman, and had assassinated Jackson. Police had discovered evidence that London, who is white, blacked out his face like a commando and wore an Afro wig to the shooting site of Jackson and Voye. Police retrieved a duffel bag belonging to London that yielded the wig and some dark theatrical makeup. London, a member of Tribal Thumb, was a close associate of the group's founder, Earl Satcher. Satcher was an early suspect in the killings but was not indicted."

★ ★ ★

I pushed through the revolving brass doors of our office building like a hamster in a wheel, flung out to the shadowy steep fjords of the financial district. I walked across the brick plaza, past the bronze figures on the Mechanics Monument who were struggling like the Marines in the famous Iwo Jima monument. It was a typical white-sky summer day in San Francisco, the kind of day you finally bring in your laundry; it's been hanging out two or three days, and it's almost dry. A breeze off the bay swooped up the wide slot of Market Street, blowing papers and sandy grit and making Styrofoam cups do whirligigs in the gutters.

I looked down Market for the trolley. The clock on the Ferry Building said 12:10. Several old green Muni buses waddled up the street, hanging from a tangled grid of electrical wires. A toothless old man stood in the center of the plaza, shouting, "I want *money!*" After a minute, he tottered over to sit on the wide marble steps of the old Crocker Bank, looking worn out from his efforts.

On my lunch hour, I had to pick up two things: Sally's purse and some clothing at the Hall of Justice and her car at the auto yard in the Mission where the police had sent it for repairs. The electric bus swayed out from the curb, groaning like a tired camel at its passengers. I sat on a scarred seat near the back exit, next to a window. The bus smelled like old popcorn, like Woolworths. At the next stop, the driver pulled away from the curb just as two young men ran up to the door. One of them pounded on it, yelling, but the driver swung the bus out into the traffic. I turned and watched as the two young men ran alongside the bus, laughing as they dropped behind. A Market Street city block is a long one.

At the next stop, the driver let an old lady on the bus and then pulled away just as the two runners puffed up to the doors. They swore and then took off again, sprinting with youth and health and outrage, and I was sure that next time, the third time, would be the charm for them; they would unlock the driver's hard heart, and he would pause in time for them to get on the bus. But no, once again, they got to the stop just a second too late. The driver, playing by his own set of rules, closed the door with a hiss. I watched them standing on the sidewalk, bending over, heaving great breaths, cursing a world that made people so small and mean. But before I would work up a real steam of outrage on their behalf, I saw them begin to laugh. On Market Street, there would always be another bus.

The San Francisco Hall of Justice is a big solid guardian of a city block. Unlike the city's architectural beauties, at risk of crumbling like sandcastles during an earthquake, the Hall of Justice would surely survive, imperiously intact. Inside, there was the busyness of a hospital, with lawyers and law enforcement instead of doctors rushing down fluorescent-lit hallways, checking their clipboards and peering into their briefcases. A lawyer conferred with a family in a tight circle; people lounged on benches, waiting to judge or be judged. Some sipped cardboard-scented coffee. Smokers were quarantined together like lepers in a glass-enclosed designated smoking area.

I took the elevator to Homicide on the fourth floor. The inspector assigned to the case handed me a receipt to retrieve Sally's belongings from the evidence room down in the building's basement. The inspector talked of the investigation but had nothing to add to what had been printed in the papers. He gave off intensity like cologne, even when listening. We stood in the reception area; phones rang in distant rooms.

"Sally was such a pretty girl," he said. "She was in the wrong place at the wrong time." I nodded, but I was annoyed. Investigators and the media had kept up this mantra, trying to reduce the murders to their simplest terms. Sally was depicted as naive, yet I knew she was anything but gullible. She had a well-developed bullshit radar. I swore silently and turned to go down to the basement. Just then, a man came through the doorway and handed the inspector a stack of photographs. The inspector put the photos on a desk. From where I was, they were upside down, but I could see the outline of Sally's car.

"We got these really great color pictures of them in the car," he said with obvious pride. "They really show what happened. But . . ." He lifted the stack of pictures to his chest. "I guess you wouldn't . . ."

"Please, no . . ." I felt bile rising in my throat, a taste of brass. I stepped toward the door. I needed oxygen. I was like a sparrow knocked senseless by a broad clear window. I lurched down the hall and hit the elevator button with a shaky finger.

On one side of the basement was a cafeteria, and facing it was a caged-in evidence and property room. Behind the counter were rows of metal racks filled with cardboard boxes, paper bags, guns, and clothes, each item tagged and numbered. The officer on duty took my receipt and handed me a paper bag with Sally's name on it. I returned to the ground floor past a line of people who were waiting to be frisked for weapons before entering the building. Outside in the watery sunlight, I sat on a concrete retaining wall and opened the bag.

I saw Sally's blue poncho and her purse. There was no blouse, and I knew why it was missing: *five bullets in the back and head*. When I opened her purse, broken car window glass rained all over my lap and spilled onto the sidewalk, the small round pieces rolling like uncut diamonds. Her wallet still had a five- and a one-dollar bill in it. Pictures of me and the rest of the family smiled from behind the cloudy plastic windows, as well as her driver's license, a credit card, and a card with her blood type. I put everything back into the bag and made a little roll at the top, like a bag lunch, reminding me that I was hungry, but there would be no time to stop for a bite; I had to go further, deep into the Mission District.

Back on the bus, I held the brown sack in my lap, cradling it with both hands as if it held the treasures of an ancient civilization. The police had given me the address of the place where Sally's car was being fixed. Sally loved that gold Camaro. It had been impounded for days until it had been exhausted of all clues, and then it was sent out for repairs.

The auto repair lot was a block off Valencia. I had lived for years in San Francisco, but this was a neighborhood that I had never visited. I would figure out later that it was only a few blocks from where Sally had been murdered, but I had no desire to go there yet. I walked through an opening in the chain-link fence. I could see Sally's car at the far end behind other cars as if it were a horse not wanting to be caught. A piece of yellow paper under the windshield wiper flapped in the wind. I stepped inside a tiny shack that served as an office and gave the man there my receipt. His name plate said his name was Tony. He lifted Sally's keys and asked me to wait on the sidewalk while he moved other cars to get to Sally's.

Out at the curb, I wondered if I should even drive. I felt so woozy and out of focus. I didn't really want to get into Sally's car; it would always be a crime scene. I never wanted to see it again. But somebody had to step up, be strong. Dad had a buyer lined up for the car already; the car was only two years old. I didn't know who was buying it. Had he put an ad in the paper? "Gold Camaro, lo miles, gd condition, minor holes in upholstery . . ." Probably not.

Tony roared up to the curbside and leaped out. He grinned, obviously pleased with his workmanship. The motor was running, he was double-parked, and I had no choice but to get into the car. But for a moment, I was immobile—what if there is blood . . . The paper bag was damp from my grip, rolled and limp like an old magazine at a dentist's office.

I forced myself to look in, my stomach boiling. But the car looked perfect. The windshield and window glass had been replaced, the seats had been repaired, and the little diamonds of safety glass had been vacuumed out of all crevices. I could smell carpet shampoo.

I was more unnerved than if there had been gore. She's gone, vanished. I knew I was standing on the corner too long; my feet felt connected to the pavement like a monument. Tony was holding the door open, shifting from one foot to the other. He had to get back to work. I had to get back to work. Still, I stood, tears backing up behind my eyes, held in by surface tension; the first tear out would cause a tidal wave.

Then inside the car, my view focused on a gap in the dash where the radio had been. "Where's the radio?" I asked.

"I dunno. The radio was gone when we got the car," he said.

I erupted. "Where's the goddamned radio!" I shouted. "How could anyone rob the dead! I'm gonna tell the homicide inspectors about this, and if you had anything to do with it . . . It didn't get taken at the police impound lot!" Tony was no longer smiling; he glowered in a scary way.

I didn't want to be strong. I wanted to be weak, like the sparrow knocked askew by the glass window. Couldn't anybody put me in a towel-lined shoebox, hold me in their hand, and feed me with an eyedropper until I could fly again? I threw the limp bag into the back seat, slammed myself into the gold Camaro casket, and joined the flow of traffic on Valencia Street.

For Tony, proud of his upholstery repair; for the inspector with his great photos; for the cruel bus driver, it was all in a day's work. Only I was overwhelmed with sorrow and rage. I fumed all the way across the bridge. The hives were beginning to itch. I dropped the car at my parents', and we never talked about where it finally went; it vanished like a ghost.

★ ★ ★

I wanted to understand Sally's relationship with Popeye Jackson. The newspaper photos showed him to be a not particularly attractive forty-five-year-old black man who apparently had been in prison several times since he was about twenty-five. And what was up with the dorky name? In the few photos I had seen, his eyes looked like anyone else's. His crimes were burglary and robbery and drug possession. He had been paroled in 1970, and for the five years before his death, he had been active in prisoners' rights organizations before finally forming his own, which he called the United Prisoners Union. He had married Pat Singer in 1973. I didn't know when Sally met him, but it was probably 1973 or '74. One of her friends said they had met at a prison literacy program at San Quentin where she was volunteering.

I go to the *San Francisco Chronicle* archives to the period before the murders. Apparently, in 1973, Popeye was arrested for possession of heroin and marijuana that was found in his car. He claimed they were planted by police, and at trial in November of 1973, he said he would *never* have had heroin because he had "strong anti-drug feelings because his son was born suffering from heroin addiction withdrawals, because his wife [at the time] had been using heroin during her pregnancy." Also, a testimony by a paid informant who volunteered at the United Prisoners Union was contradictory and unreliable. She first said she drove Popeye's car to the police for inspection without his knowledge, of course. Later, she recanted her role, saying Tribal Thumb members had forced her to inform on Popeye. He was acquitted of the drug charges.

I began to see a little bit of what must have drawn Sally to him when I read that in April of 1974, the "charismatic" Popeye Jackson went to a parole hearing at San Quentin, and "150 supporters marched in the rain" outside the prison walls. Ultimately, thanks to Randy Hearst's support and Popeye's "work in the community," his parole was not revoked despite some shoplifting and the fact that he had been in a scuffle with police just days before the parole hearing. The scuffle had been at a fundraising rally for Popeye's defense. Sally had probably been there.

I never did find out how he got the cartoonish name Popeye. None of the few pictures I ever saw showed bulging eyes. But what had become clearer and clearer to me, if not to those investigating the murders, is that it was all about jealousy. Popeye had influential supporters. He could draw a crowd; he had charisma; he had the ear of a rich and influential man, Randolph Hearst; he had the chicks; and he got special treatment that others in his ex-convict ghetto-boy circle would never have been able to get. He had achieved a certain status. And even though it would seem that radical underground groups in a city like San Francisco could work together to achieve common goals—there were several groups working for prisoners' rights—they all hated each other. There would be no honor among thieves in the underworld of prison gangs in San Francisco.

Snitch means "to inform, tattle," as defined by the *Random House Dictionary of the English Language*. You could kill, rob banks, drug yourself, or rape and do a myriad of random acts of thuggery yet still hold your head high as a proud member of Tribal Thumb or the SLA or the United Prisoners Union. But to be a snitch, well, that was a real crime in the gang world. Apparently, all you had to do was call someone a snitch, true or not, and a death sentence was issued. Proof not required.

In a 1977 article in *Playboy*, the magazine that called itself "entertainment for men," Paul Krassner (a writer from the publication *The Realist*) wrote an article entitled "The Parts Left Out of the Patty Hearst Trial." He stated that there was a missing link between Patty Hearst and Sara Jane Moore: the murder of Wilbert "Popeye" Jackson. "The leader of the United Prisoners Union had been killed, together with a companion, Sally Voye, while they sat in a parked car at two o'clock in the morning." Krassner claimed he learned from "*impeccable sources* that the hit *was known in advance* within the California Department of Corrections, the FBI, the San Jose and San Francisco police departments." Krassner also reprinted an old statement by a "Berkeley underground group called Tribal Thumb": "It has become known to the Tribal Thumb orbit that the CIA, FBI and CCS [Criminal Conspiracy Section] have made undercurrent moves to establish a basis for the total eradication of the Tribal Thumb Community . . . [They] are involved in working overtime to unravel the mystery of Popeye Jackson's execution in an effort to plant Tribal Thumb in a web of conspiracy in that execution . . ."

Krassner wrote that the FBI's heavy involvement in the case of Popeye's death is largely due to the death of Sally Voye, "who in actuality was moonlighting (outside her employment as a teacher) as a narcotics agent for police forces. Moreover, she was Popeye's control agent," and Popeye was an informer.

Krassner continued, throwing out still another "theory," saying that Popeye Jackson could have been killed by police agents "to neutralize yet another black leader, rather than because he was supposed to be an informer . . ."

The *Playboy* article made me crazy. It was an outrage. It was not the first time I had seen in print that Tribal Thumb had called Popeye a snitch. But now my sister was being painted with the same brush and worse. I contacted Krassner by e-mail a couple of years before he died, and he stuck with his version of events and, of course, wouldn't reveal any sources. We'll never know who his "impeccable sources" were. So many insects had crawled out of the underground to either claim responsibility or deny the killings. They wanted a chance to give voice to their opinions about the crime and, of course, get up on a soapbox to air their overall worldview. The *Playboy* article was in early 1977. In April of that year, Tribal Thumb's founder and guru, Earl Satcher (who was another of the volunteers for the PIN food giveaway), was shot to death in a gunbattle in Hunter's Point. It had been rumored that he had ordered the hit on Popeye and his fellow Thumbster Richard London complied, perhaps with one or more accomplices. Despite the leadership void left by Satcher's murder, over the next decade, members of the Tribal Thumb gang of criminals would carry on, committing crimes involving explosives, firearms, mail fraud, bank robbery, jailbreaks, and murder.

And we all know that the SLA "army" vaporized after Patty Hearst was finally found in September of 1975. Patty Hearst had been found guilty of bank robbery while in the clutches of the SLA. But she served a pittance of prison time, two years of a seven-year sentence, before President Jimmy Carter commuted her sentence, and she was released. (She actually received a full pardon from President Bill Clinton in 2001.)

Two years after his arrest, London went on trial for the two murders of Popeye Jackson and Sally. Mom and Dad went to the trial every day. Mom said she wanted to see what was said about Sally. "I just have to go I want to find out if they drag her name through the mud," she said. She told me nothing "damaging to her reputation" had been said during the trial. A jailhouse informant testified that London bragged to him that he was a member of a three-man hit team. "Sally was there, and because she was there, she had to go," London apparently said.

Dad had retreated into a haze of alcohol those days. I had just given birth to our daughter Elizabeth, so it was out of the question for me to attend the trial, and the truth was, I did not want to go. I would be seeing the murderer, and if he had a smile on his face or was idly doodling with a pencil, I feared I wouldn't be able to control the urge to scream at or attack his sorry ass.

What seemed in the early days of the investigation to be a lone gunman had, in fact, according to prosecutors, been the action of two, maybe three shooters. Even though the young witness described a slender man running from the crime scene, not two men, there was a second gun in the investigators' reports. At trial, the prosecution said there were bullets from both a 9-millimeter and a .38-caliber automatic. Two guns, so probably two shooters? And there was evidence of a third, perhaps a getaway driver. Court documents revealed that London even claimed he was the shooter in only one of the two killings—which one? Did he kill Sally or Popeye? Could someone like that be trusted to tell the truth, ever? Finally, London was convicted and sentenced to life in prison.

In 1980, the *Chronicle* reported that London's appeal was denied. London claimed that evidence used in his trial had been seized in illegal searches. The evidence included the short black Afro wig and dark theatrical makeup, evidence that apparently convinced the jury of his guilt.

★★★

Dad always said he hated weeding, funerals, churches, and horses. Why horses? He'd been sent as a kid every summer to a ranch in Eastern Oregon that was owned by friends of his parents. He knew all about horses, riding them, feeding them, mucking out their stalls. He developed this loathing for horses, he said, because they were so dumb. I thought this prejudice against horses was unfair. They were beautiful and majestic, and I loved them. Mom and Dad laughed at that, at my longing for a horse. When we were in middle school, Sally and I and neighbors Lynn and Annette started saving all our allowance and babysitting money to buy a horse. Dad just about fell off his chair laughing at us when he found out. "Where are you going to put it? In the backyard?" he roared. By Thanksgiving, it was clear that we wouldn't be able to buy a horse; just $10 had been accumulated, and at that rate, it would take us until we were in our thirties, and we had to admit that by then, we probably wouldn't be wanting to own a portion of a horse. So Lynn's mom (who had volunteered to hold our purse) suggested we use the money to buy a basket of food for a needy family that year. An article in the *Menlo Park Recorder* said, "Youngsters' Spirit of Thanksgiving." In 1954, the $10 would actually buy a Thanksgiving dinner. Smiles in the accompanying photo look a bit forced.

When Dad went on about how dumb horses were, I thought, OK then, if a horse is too dumb, do we need to have a pet with a high IQ? How about a chimp or a colobus monkey? Ironically, in Alamo, when we first moved in, we had a neighbor who actually had a monkey. It lived outside, chained to a tree. Mom made the mistake of stepping inside the radius of the chain's circle, and it flew from its tree, screaming, and landed on her shoulder and bit her on the side of the neck. It was smart, all right. We opted for cuddly; we had devoted dogs and cats, and they were usually as smart as God intended them to be.

What Dad really loved was his family, his work, and the 49ers (he'd had season tickets since the team's inception in the late 1940s; the team's first quarterback was a Stanford fraternity brother), and he loved drinking and talking and laughing and telling stories. He'd sit in the family room and be entertained by all four of his kids' adventures. The bar was usually open at our house, and there was laughter. By the time we were in Alamo, my brother had already, even in middle school, become a talented athlete, and Dad loved going to his baseball, football, and basketball games right up through Rob's high school. Rob and his friends were particularly amusing, and Dad would laugh until he cried, blowing his nose in great bursts, groaning and sighing. "We had Joe going for the hankie," they would say. After college, Rob and his friends played in a softball league.

Their team was called the Snoids, named for a cartoon character invented by R. Crumb, a counterculture cartoonist. A snoid could live in the mountains, but they could also live in women's rectums. Snoids were OK with that because they only had to vacate a couple of times a day, and the rent was cheap.

When I was in college in 1966, Mom and Dad bought a summer cabin at Lake of the Woods, about thirty-five miles from Dad's old hometown, Klamath Falls. We had vacationed there for a couple of years in rented quarters, and we all loved the lake. Our cabin and its outhouse (dubbed The Wee Hoosie) had been built in the 1930s by a teacher at Dad's high school. The cabin came complete with furniture, bedding, a chandelier made out of a boat anchor, and a wood-burning stove. There was even an old homemade mahogany motorboat in the boathouse and water skis made of wood, with tennis shoes nailed to them. The boat was winched into and out of the boathouse on a wooden dolly on railroad tracks. After only a couple of trips around the lake, the boat sank at our dock and was eventually hauled away. Dad replaced it with a yellow fiberglass boat that we all zoomed behind for waterskiing and for slo-mo cruising around the lake.

Dad was a finance man, trained as an accountant, and his facility with numbers partly explained how he could always win at cards. At the lake, there were usually at least three of us kids, plus some of Rob and Anne's friends would come stay, sleeping on the porch or on the dock, even sometimes in the bed of their pickup trucks. In addition, Mom and Dad had friends from Klamath Falls who had their own cabins around the lake. Dad loved that there were plenty of victims for his card triumphs, especially the game called Hearts. He would "shoot the moon," quietly gathering all the hearts, taking the queen of spades, laughing and gloating as it became clear to the other players that once again, he had them skunked. He would exult in pure joy as the other players grumbled and plotted their revenge in another round.

Dad also was a champion at ping-pong. We had a table set up on our covered patio in Menlo Park so we could play year-round. In Alamo, the ping-pong table was in the garage. Dad put a mean topspin on the ball that was my nemesis. He could beat all of us without putting down his cocktail or even spilling it. Sally and I played often, trying to get good enough to beat Dad. Finally, it took years, but I did get good enough that I could beat him, occasionally, by a few points only.

Before my wedding, I spent four days in my old bedroom in Alamo to help with the food; have a final fitting of my bridal gown, which Grandmother made (she also made the three bridesmaids dresses); and help with the garden. Really, Mom did most of it, but I did lend a hand. Two days before the wedding, Sally showed up, and we all had dinner together. After dinner though, she said she was going out, with no explanation. I thought about how we had grown apart after she took her fifth year at Berkeley for her teaching credential. Her crowd spent a surprising amount of time at meetings, marches, and demonstrations. Didn't anybody besides me have to get up each day and be at work early, then shop for dinner, cook it, eat, and fall into bed? Schoolteachers did seem to have more time off than ordinary mortals, but as Sally frequently reminded me, they earned it. At my workplace, we got two weeks or, if we worked there for more than ten years, three weeks of vacation per year. The only time she visited me at my office, during her summer break, when I introduced her to the president of the company, she took the opportunity to tell him that two weeks were not nearly enough time for a proper vacation.

Finally, I saw headlights shine on the ceiling and throw a gridded shadow on the Venetian blinds. I heard the patio door slide open and the dog's nails click as he greeted her at the door. She carefully tiptoed up the stairs. "Where have you been?" I whispered from my bed. She answered, "I've been to an Al-Anon meeting. It's for family members of alcoholics." She went into the bathroom to brush her teeth, and the door was rimmed with gold from the light inside. I thought for a long time in the dark while she readied for bed. At what point in your life do your roles reverse and you start being the parent to your parents?

When she came out and turned out the light, I said, "Don't you think that's—" and she cut in, "Drastic? Hardly. Everybody knows Dad is pie-eyed every night, and nobody does anything! Well, I am going to *try*." She hissed into the darkness. I knew she could confront; she could recognize a situation for what it was, not for what it used to be or pretended to be. She could point the impolite finger at unfairness. "He needs help," she said, turning over to sleep, my maid of honor. She was wrong, of course. None of us could help Dad; he had to want to help himself. But she wanted to do something.

★ ★ ★

Bruce pulls away in our car to search for a parking place, leaving me to enter the country club lounge alone. "Welcome Class of 1963," reads a banner, shiny as tinfoil, with long silver streamers hanging down. It's our twentieth high school reunion. Helium balloons roost on the ceiling, and crepe paper twists its way across the dance floor ringed with tables. A band is setting up speakers and moving instruments around on a low stage. Air-conditioned air is whooshing through the vents above. People start to stream in from the parking lot, some of the men paunchier and balder than the last reunion. Many of the women, thanks to makeup and hair coloring, look good still.

I can see a bartender cutting limes at the long bar on the side of the room. He bends like a surgeon at his work, and I feel weak; these are dangerous days of my sobriety. My days are filled with effort as I try not to dream of the spicy taste of Bombay gin swirled with fizzy tonic and the smell of fresh cut lime. I shut off the thought of the heft of a thick, strong glass, frosted and icy, promising a slow inner journey. Or the perfume, the nose, of red wine and how warm it tastes with meat, how it enhances the earthy purity of cheese, of bread. Or champagne, how I used to lift my goblet high at weddings, like an Olympian carrying the eternal flame, how the silver bubbles exploded against the sky of my mouth.

Bruce walks over, and we line up to get our name tags. Sandy and Donna, neither of whom I was particularly close to in high school, organize the name tags as we walk over to the bar. Name tags are key at these reunions, and they better be printed in an extra large font. Funny how you think you knew everybody in your class at school, and the class wasn't huge, yet at reunions, someone greets you that you have no memory of. We sit in the cool white noise of the air-conditioning and stare out the dark-tinted windows at the sculpted green turf. Bruce orders gin and tonic; I order Perrier. Tonight, or ever, I won't be loud or lurching around or puking in the bathroom. My compass has been reset. I don't need the social lubrication of alcohol. Actually, I am perfectly capable of making a fool out of myself without it.

It's not fair. Jesus drank wine, and we know he turned water into it. "Drink this, in remembrance of me," Jesus said. "It is my blood."

I think about how the first alcohol might have been discovered—it must have been a mistake, like the camel milk that accidentally became yogurt after a long sloshing in a goatskin bag across the desert in the heat. I can just imagine those first cave dwellers. He: "Woman! This barley water looks funny." She: "Sorry, I left it behind the fire, and it got all fizzy like that, but it's all we have. We must drink it." The next morning, they awake with pounding heads, recalling the laughter and dancing, and invite neighboring cave dwellers over to the first cocktail party in recorded history.

I sip my Perrier. I actually feel great not drinking. But drinking still is a constant temptation that I need to avoid. Dad had quit drinking for as long as I have, almost a year. His doctor said his liver was like hamburger; he would die if he took another drink. His drinking had had a cumulative effect. What began for him in high school and especially college, as recreation, an integral part of his social life, had turned into poison. So many of his college buddies' lives were similarly impacted. Dad had finally taken the doctor's advice. After a year of sobriety, Dad looked better and said he felt better, and I was proud of him.

I can still see Dad, weeks before his death, back in June, 1980. We were in Alamo, sitting outside at an umbrella table, watching my two-year-old daughter play on the steps of the pool, water wings on her arms. The early summer was buzzing with crickets singing in the tawny grass beyond the fence. Mom had gone to the store. We had just finished a sandwich, and Dad went back into the house to get the glass he had left in the kitchen. On the table where I sat was a favorite book from my childhood that I had been reading to my daughter Elizabeth earlier. It was called *My Father's Dragon*.

I watched through the sliding glass doors as Dad moved slowly into the kitchen. Earlier, some friends had stopped by, and he fixed them drinks, but not for himself. I could see him picking up several glasses, sniffing them, and putting them down before finding the one that was his, the one that was safe, with pure iced tea. All but his were laced with poison. He dipped his beak into each glass, so careful, so aware of the danger. But just a few weeks after that visit, Dad took his final drink like Socrates. He and Mom would go to the cabin at the lake the following week, and I would never see him again.

★ ★ ★

My head floats like a beach ball on top of the tepid water of the pool, my toes on the bottom. It's nine o'clock on a hot August night, the sky is black, and my father has died in Klamath Falls, his birthplace. Mom sits in a patio chair, her ankles crossed, her fingers drawing in the dust on the glass top of the umbrella table. She's taken care of everything; the fat cardboard box of his ashes is already strewn into the Pacific Ocean according to Dad's wishes. Her eyes seem to search the table for the right words. She is telling me how my father died. "Oh, he ruined his health from the drinking." I think, yes, cirrhosis of the liver will put a real dent in your health.

She sighs. "He fixed himself this killer drink," she says, stifling a sob. Her choice of words is spot on. We both know it wasn't suicide, but . . . She continues, "After he drank it, he started wandering 'round the cabin. He'd sit down, stand up, walk out to the porch, and he would groan." I wondered if he was in pain or if it was the sort of groan you do when you've made a terrible mistake. His doctor told him any more drinking would kill him, but he did it anyway. Big mistake.

I push off the bottom of the pool with my big toe and float for a while on my back. Mom is silent, looking at the dark water of the pool. I can't understand; he had been doing so well. I can see stars glittering above the far mountains. A breeze is starting to swish though the tall redwood trees that stand shoulder to shoulder along the fence. Some bratty neighbor kids a year ago had a habit of throwing dirt clods over that fence into our pool until Dad had a stern talk with their parents. Their last name was Jerko. Dad said you can't even make that name up. Truly. I study the dark sequined sky, wishing I had paid attention in science class when we were studying constellations. I think I see the Big Dipper. Is that Orion's Belt? I see billions of stars. Note to self: Find a book to help me understand the night sky. But the sky would hold no answer to my father's addiction.

Mom said she couldn't get Dad to talk to her that night. He couldn't seem to hear her. It was as if he'd gone into a coma but was still ambulatory. She managed to get him, still groaning, into the car (still no phone at our summer cabin) and drove the thirty-five miles to the hospital in Klamath Falls. The hospital was named for a big donor, one of the two other partners of the long-defunct Big Lakes Box Company, of which Dad's father had been the third partner and general manager. Dad got oxygen, intravenous nutrients, around-the-clock care, and no alcohol. It worked for a couple of days, but after a lifetime of booze-filled days, the cumulative effect of years and years of hard drinking, he slipped into a coma and died four days later. He was sixty years old.

I never went to see him in that hospital. Mom was so sure that Dad would recover, and since I had a toddler daughter to care for, I shouldn't make the seven-hour trip to Klamath Falls. Rob and Anne did go; they were students off for the summer. This wasn't Dad's first trip to the hospital with liver problems. Mom said he had a "strong constitution." Not strong enough, apparently. Rob called me; once again, he was the caller with bad news.

"Pop died," he said, and I wailed, Mom didn't know how bad the cirrhosis had gotten; none of us did. As children in Dad's house, we didn't suffer because of his drinking. He never got angry or hit anyone. He was never arrested for drunk driving. Instead, drinking made him happy, made him laugh and appreciate things that were funny. He could talk, really talk, and he could listen. And all the time, Dad told us he loved us.

I cry into the dark water of the pool, wishing I had driven those long hours against Mom's advice. I could have endured the diapers, the blubbering in the car seat, the frequent stops for playing and snacking with a two-year-old. For a last glimpse of my Dad, it would have been worth it. I look straight up at the spangled sky and think of the small blue tattoo of a star on Dad's upper arm—his souvenir of his time in the Marines. In high school, a couple of my friend's boyfriends had seen it at the edge of his T-shirt sleeve and started calling him Star.

1989

I was on my way to Vallejo to find a memorial bench. I'd dropped the kids at school and blasted across the Richmond–San Rafael Bridge. I had the name of Sally's school but no map. If my husband had been involved with this trip, there would have been a map with the route highlighted in yellow. At the Carquinez Bridge, I had to stop and pay a toll. A small black youth perched on a chair inside the toll booth, his hand out, his eyes trained on the thick textbook resting on his lap. I could not see if it was American History or Intro to Biology. He thanked me for the forty cents, and I admired his dedication to his education, the struggle to study under the relentless interruption.

I took the first Vallejo exit, hoping the school where Sally had taught would just appear before me. After a few minutes of driving around, I knew I needed to ask directions. I found one that looked not too busy and parked by the restrooms.

"Help ya?" said a man with "Ray" embroidered on his shirt and a can of Prestone in his hand. "I'm looking for Federal School," I said. Ray poked a grimy finger at a tiny schoolhouse with a red flag on a map of Vallejo that was tacked to the wall. "It's over across town, by the housing projects," he said. He told me how best to get there, and I thanked him and left.

Federal School was surrounded by a housing project on the margin of Vallejo's deep water ship channel. The project was actually two-story townhouse apartments, with rows of beige doors set in beige concrete blocks, each with a coil of green garden hose underneath the cement stoop.

Parallel lines for hanging out laundry hung like telegraph lines connecting each building. A pair of stiff new blue jeans rumpled on one of the lines like an old cormorant drying its wings. No doubt a number of the occupants worked as welders and fiberglass experts and marine electricians at the Mare Island Naval Shipyard nearby.

I parked and followed the sidewalk to the front door of the school. It was a single-story buff-colored sandstone building with an ArtDeco roundness to its corners and a thirties-style lettering announcing its name over the doors. It took up a whole block.

My sneakers squeaked on the shiny floor as I walked to the principal's office. I could smell overcooked coffee and disinfectant. The school secretary was typing on an old manual typewriter. She dabbed correction fluid on her paper and blew on it as I explained the reason for my visit.

"My sister taught school here about fifteen years ago, and I'm looking for a memorial bench that someone told me was here . . ."

"Hmm, I've only been here seven years," she said with a perky smile. "I don't know of anything like that. Sorry."

I grimaced. Why did I wait so long to come here? Denial, resentment, and procrastination all played a part. There never would be a right time to come here; there would never be "closure" or understanding. I turned to leave.

"Say," she said, "why don't you call Edna Tompkins. She was the principal here for years. She still lives in town. Here's her number." I took the piece of paper and returned to my car.

I found a pay phone at a mini market and called Edna Tompkins. "Hello?" said a well-worn voice. I quickly explained I was looking for Sally's memorial bench. "Oh yes, honey, I remember Sally. That was years ago. I'm retired now, you know. She was a fine teacher. She taught first grade." She stopped. "But I don't know about any bench."

"I thought she taught kindergarten." I was confused.

"At Federal, she taught first. But she was transferred over to Loma Vista. She had a kindergarten class over there, honey, when she uh, passed away."

I got directions and emerged from the urine-smelling phone booth with some hope. Sally had taught at two different Vallejo schools, and maybe the bench was at this second one. I drove along streets named for states, past proud Victorian homes as grand as anything in San Francisco. I entered a post–World War II residential area where most of the small flat-roofed homes reminded me of my childhood home in the 1940s in Menlo Park on Ashton Street.

Loma Vista School occupied the top of a small hill—I remembered that *loma* meant hill from my Spanish classes. There was a faraway vista of the water, silvered now in the cool sun. The school was painted an unfortunate color of bright blue, probably visible from outer space.

Before entering the hallway, I quickly scanned the play yard. No bench. I explained to another perky secretary in the office about my search for the bench, which I had a faint memory that it had been in a grove of redwoods, someone years ago had said. She said I needed to wait for the principal, and I was not encouraged when she said the principal was fairly new.

The principal was talking on the phone in a room stenciled Principal, the same kind of stenciled lettering you see at military installations or on equipment. Top Secret, No Admittance, or No Step on the wings of airplanes. After a long wait, during which I used a room marked "Toilet – Girls," I began to get restless. Soon it would be time for me to pick up my own children from school. The principal's voice continued behind her door.

An older woman entered from the corridor. "Oh, Norma, maybe you can help this lady. You've worked here a long time," the secretary said. Norma set down a large piece of tagboard. "Seventeen years." Norma smiled, turning to me.

Norma nodded her head as I explained about Sally and the bench. "Yes, I remember Sally," Norma said. "I was an aide in her classroom for a while." She picked up the tagboard, pushed open the door with her rear end, and gave a jerky motion with her head to indicate that I should follow her out into the yard.

It was recess now, and the yard was filled with children running, screaming, and throwing balls around the playground. It was like looking through a kaleidoscope, all bright colors moving in my peripheral vision. Norma was pointing to a couple of redwoods which were the only break in the flat, hard-packed earth and blacktop of the playground.

"There did used to be a bench," Norma said. "It was there until three, maybe four years ago. It just sort of rotted away, and the maintenance supervisor wouldn't let it stay, all splintery like that . . . Kids could get hurt. There were more trees too once, but well . . . you know how kids are." She turned to me. "You know, Sally was such a good person. It was such a great loss, so unnecessary."

I struggled against tears; I had been hoping I wouldn't cry. When *was* a murder necessary? The bell sounded, and the maelstrom of children swooped into the building like metal filings to a magnet, and the yard became silent. I thanked Norma and walked back to my car. I looked back one last time to the scraggly redwoods struggling to live in such a dry environment; I knew they thrived in the cool foggy coast where they could live for hundreds of years. *Sequoia sempervirens*—always alive.

★ ★ ★

I'm driving across the Golden Gate Bridge to San Francisco. In the rearview mirror, I can see the lumpy headlands of Marin, my own home a microdot in the sun-toasted hills. I drive past the woolly *maquis* growing on the Marin Headlands, the same kind of shrubbery that concealed and gave its name to the French underground guerrilla fighters that fought the Nazis during World War II. I grip the wheel with a renewal of my purpose. Ahead, fog is blowing across the bridge, blotting out all color, making everything, patterns and shadows, shifting like a film noir.

I traverse Lombard and then Van Ness, the double-barreled boulevard that shoots straight and clean into the Mission District where I want to go: Albion Street, where Sally was murdered. I've been to see the memorial bench in Vallejo, and it's time that I visit the scene of her death. The traffic is slow and thick like syrup, cars clotting intersections and hardening in the arterials. I pass automobile showrooms like mausoleums; do people still come here, with all this congestion, to purchase a car? Could you even get the sense of a car on a test drive here, stuck in traffic?

I pass the San Francisco City Hall, where I once worked a temporary job in the sheriff's office. Each day, I typed receipts (called warrants) with three carbons on an old manual typewriter. These were the fees that people had to pay to file a civil complaint against a dry cleaner, a landlord, or a flaky tenant. After a few months of that, I got a better job down on Montgomery Street in the financial district.

I see so many changes in this neighborhood. There is a burger joint in a building that looks rounded and curvaceous like the Guggenheim Museum in New York. There's the Louise Davies Concert Hall, where there used to be an old stale dive bar called the Jury Room where lawyers and prosecutors socialized with martinis. Behind this block, facing the end of the freeway, there are condominiums where there used to be a dusty row of Victorian buildings. A sign in one of the windows used to say "Quiet - Day Sleeper." Right. It must have been like trying to sleep on an airport runway, cars endlessly funneling off the freeway and gunning their engines for the steep rise of Franklin Street.

I was a day sleeper too for some of my work life. I had a variety of office jobs that were so boring I might have been able to have done them asleep. In the early 1970s, I lived with four friends from college in a flat on Pine Street. We took the electric buses down to the financial district (me) or to the Civic Center (Lauren who worked at the passport office) or to mid–Market Street, where Kathy and Melanie worked at the Emporium as assistant buyers. Barbara was a teacher, and I did envy her; it was a job with real commitment, like Sally had. I took temp jobs but refused to believe that my temp assignments could become permanent, a career even; it was prison with pay, mostly involving a phone and a typewriter. At one of the stodgy financial firms on Montgomery Street, I wore slacks to work for the two-week gig, and at the end, several of the women thanked me for wearing pants—something they dared not do until I came along and broke through that ceiling so they could wear pants to work as well.

I recall how keen I was to learn to type. In eighth grade at Oak Knoll School, typing was offered as an elective. You had to bring your own typewriter. Off I went three times a week, balancing this big, heavy black manual typewriter on the handlebars of my bicycle. And of course, I had to bring it home again so I could practice. Sally and I would sit at our desks, doing homework, and I would ask her to time me for my typing test. "Ready, set, go!" she'd say, setting Mom's kitchen timer, and I would type like a maniac. After a few weeks of this, she said, "Ready, set, Google!" and I couldn't type because of laughing. We both found *Google* to be an impossibly funny word. We couldn't imagine that a company with that funny name would someday be a world power. Or that just about everybody learned to type, without lessons, thanks to personal computers and iPhones.

I didn't really want to be a teacher, but those long holidays and entire indolent summers sure had appeal. "You'd be in it for all the wrong reasons," Sally snapped at me once when I said I might go to grad school for a teaching credential. She was right, but I didn't want to hear about it. "God, she drove me crazy," I say out loud as I drive underneath the freeway at the foot of Van Ness. I'm in the Mission District now.

It's the neighborhood of Mission Dolores: the pains in Spanish, the wounds. Sally died near Mission Dolores, and I am going to see where it happened. I try not to think about her wounds: *five bullets in the back and head* . . . As I drive south, on Valencia Street now, the streets become more and more clogged with traffic, and walkers spill off the sidewalks at every corner. Buildings lean in, crowded, fighting for sunlight in this straight up and down city. Drivers honk; you have to have a horn that works in this neighborhood. Buses stop in the middle of the street because someone has parked in the bus stop. Cars double-park in front of stores and sit, engines running, flashers blazing, as if it's an emergency; it is, I guess, when you just gotta have cigarettes or diapers, and you can't find a parking place.

I pass a burger joint on a corner. "For a Bun on the Run," the sign says. A waitress wearing red high-top roller skates is gliding around in the parking area, with a loaded tray, her buns on the run.

I'm looking for the street where Sally died, Albion Street. It's been so many years. I don't really know why I'm here now, instead of years ago, but I guess my wounds healed so slowly, it's as if where I was pierced is finally drawing together, just as I am drawn to this place. I lived in the city on the Marina side for almost two years after Sally died, and even after we moved to Marin, I was within twenty minutes' drive, but I never wanted to come here; it was as if I blamed this jumbled, jittery city for the crime.

I have a Thomas Brothers map, but with no copilot, I'm flummoxed by which streets are one-way, and I keep getting caught behind farting buses. Albion Street now has a sort of gravitational pull that is propelling me along. *Albion* is an ancient name for England. It is off Guerrero Street, Spanish for warrior or fighter. Now I'm on numbered streets; there's such a security in knowing what street comes after Thirteenth. Finally, I spot the sign for Albion. I feel like I've just been zapped with a cattle prod. I go around the block, nowhere to park. Do Not Enter. I'm getting sweaty. No Parking, No Stopping, Tow-Away, Buses Only. Albion looks to be only a couple of blocks long, T-boned with an even smaller street, an alley really, called Camp Street.

I read somewhere that the corner of Albion and Camp streets is the historical site of the first Mission Dolores.

Cars are parked along the curbs, on the sidewalks, wrapped around corners, their tires dipping into the storm drains. I'm so hot, though the day is pleasantly cool. I've been around and around the blocks now. I'm edgy, and I almost hit two pedestrians who stride across the street at the corner, glowering at me. I cruise Valencia, Guerrero, Albion again, around and around, anxious to be on foot, but I can't find parking to save my life. I spot a car leaving and roar up behind, only to find that he was parked in the red by a fire hydrant. An old man sees me searching and motions me like a railroad conductor to wait for his spot. I honk in gratitude; I've already caught on to the street argot. I pull to the curb in front of a bookstore called Maelstrom.

I dig coins out of my purse for the meter. But my parking spot benefactor even left me with eighteen minutes on the meter. I walk around the corner, planting my feet in the center of each sidewalk square, for luck. Next door to the bookstore is Ben's Karate and Tax Service. I picture myself entering the shop and dear Ben, the proprietor, trying to figure if he should greet me wearing his black belt or his green eyeshade.

I stand underneath the street sign that says Albion Street. It's really somewhat of a back alley. Buildings are graffitied and moldy looking. Litter blows in the street, and there is dogshit on the sidewalks. The door to Conway's Funeral Home is open, and I detour in there just to see what a funeral parlor looks like. I've never been in one because my family doesn't do that. Funerals are a total mystery to me. It is silent like a church. I see several rooms for services; one is done up with crosses, while another is plain and non-committal. The manager shows me a chapel dominated by a huge fireplace with a fake stone facade of a castle on it. He explains that his grandfather came from Ireland and this is a replica of a castle there. Cooking utensils hang inside the fireplace on a wrought-iron hanger. Inside the fireplace is some genuine peat, all covered with dust and cobwebs, that his grandfather cut out of the Ould Sod and brought here for authenticity.

I blink as I emerge onto the street again. I don't know where Sally's car was parked, but I'm sure that if I walk down both sides of the entire street, I will have walked over what I now think of as her grave. Across from a bar where a mural shows three people with green faces is another mural. It depicts the Mission Reds, a team that played in the 1920s according to a sign on the mural. They played at Woodward's Amusement Park, where Valencia Gardens Housing Projects are now. Valencia Gardens—the newspaper articles said the murderer ran there after the shooting . . .

The wind blows a napkin around my ankles. I detour again, up some stairs to a flat that is having a garage sale. It's all nothing-colored carpet and wood floors crunchy with mouse droppings. Water stains decorate the ceiling, and it's not even the top floor. A Kingston Trio record album lies on a table. I leaf through a book of poetry by Rod McKuen—remember him? The woman having the sale says he lived nearby for a time. I find in the book poems about the neighborhood, and I am surprised at how the poet sees beauty and charm where I see despair and poverty.

I realize that the street numbers are in the hundreds, and I need to find number 43. Shit, I'm on the wrong block. I also realize my eighteen minutes are up. I need to get back to Marin and pick up my son from school. I don't belong here. It's as though I have held my breath for the maximum time, and I must surface to breathe. I am out of my element.

I plunge into the swift current of Mission traffic. I whizz past the Mission itself, where tourists with camera necklaces are streaming off tour buses into the Mission. A yawning sandpit with a crane, soon to become a high-rise, is very near where I picked up Sally's car so many years ago, and I saw Tony's scowling face in the rearview mirror. I turn on Franklin that will take me north out of the city. The Day Sleeper's futile request for quiet sign is long gone. Day Sleeper, I hope you found a place to rest in peace! I get over the hill, facing Marin, and suddenly I am so thankful to live in my own home with my own garage and my own backyard with roses . . . I see the tiny white triangles of sailboats on the beautiful blue bay and the peaceful beige of Angel Island. I pass Green Street where we lived for five years in a house built in the 1880s, where I lived when Sally was killed. I see the store on our corner, Hostess Market, where I bought groceries on my way home from work and Tessa would put the charges "on the book" and send us a bill at the end of the month. I loved that aspect of city life, but not the lack of parking. Across from our old flat is a small park and an Octagon House painted blue. Nothing much has changed in this neighborhood, except the tenants. They have preferential resident parking here now, but I'm not sure if it really frees up that many more spaces.

On Lombard, I pass a storefront where Marina Pizza used to be; it was the best pizza in the universe. The Italian proprietors were a big, fat lady, who wedged herself into the booth closest to the kitchen and watched a tiny TV, heaving herself into the kitchen when necessary, and her sinewy husband, who had several teeth and waited on the tables. The walls were painted with murals of the Bay of Naples. Plastic grapes hung in dusty clumps from a grid overhead. A skinny old black man with taps on his shoes came in to pick up the pizzas he delivered in the neighborhood. Some nights big mama would sing, and her voice was so rich and soulful I thought it was one of the most beautiful voices I had ever heard. Perhaps all the pounds gave her voice something to resonate from. Now they are all gone, the place is a bar with stained glass windows and ferns.

I drive back across the Golden Gate Bridge, praising the beauty of the bay with my eyes, coasting down the Waldo Grade. I feel like I just escaped from jail. It is insane to go back, but that's what I'm going to do. My mission is not accomplished. I pick up my son Brendan and blast back into the city to the Mission. "Mom, we're going around in circles," he says. "I know," I say. I had hoped he wouldn't notice and would think this was a well-planned fun outing like going to the park or the library. "I'm just trying to find a place to park."

I do find a place, this time next to Valencia Gardens. I get out feeling rather smug at having squeezed into a parking spot that may actually be smaller than my car. Some things, like bike riding and parallel parking, you never forget. I grip Brendan's hand and cross the street, entering the part of Albion Street where my sister died. The other half of Albion has some trees, but not here. I am disappointed, as if I had something to do with choosing the setting and then been overridden by some movie set director saying, "No, no, we can't have the shooting here. It's too woodsy and treesy. Over there, it's got the kind of stark hopelessness that I want to convey . . ."

This part of Albion is narrower, the houses crowd in tighter, and the cars are jam-packed together at the curbs. A couple of what are probably junkies lounge against a car, smoking something, smiling faraway smiles at nothing. I pull on Brendan's hand and hurry past. I find number 43 Albion Street and stand on the gray pavement, looking up at the three-story building. Popeye and Pat lived in the middle flat. Brendan whines,

"When are we going to the bookstore?" I smooth his hair. "We're on our way. This is a shortcut." I can hear the revving of a power drill from a car repair shop on the next street, and then it's eerily quiet. I look up at the granite steps. I see curling shingles coated with grime, dusty beveled glass with a bedsheet for a curtain. I want to absorb the atmosphere at this place; to me, it might as well be a sacred burial ground or an elephant's graveyard. Elephants never forget, do they? A man in a camouflage jacket comes out of number 43 and sits on the second to bottom of the steps, coughing and hawking and spitting into the street. I wonder if he served in Vietnam and got poisoned by Agent Orange. I move down the street, again wanting to walk down both sides, over all the sacred ground where Sally must have sat in her car, talking to Popeye. In the city, you can't assume that there would be a parking spot right in front of your building. Then again, according to the reports, the young girl could see Sally's car from her window, so I might be standing where it happened.

"Mom?" my son says. I don't answer. Down the block is a vacant lot, rare as a hot day in San Francisco. The lot sits green and pure behind a wobbly chain-link fence topped with barbed wire. The junkies are still watching us, pink eyed, like jackals. We gaze through the wire fence into the innocent unbroken ground, a punctuation in this urban wilderness. We walk past the dopers again, over the bottle caps embedded in asphalt, glittering like lost coins.

"Why are you crying?" Brendan says, looking into my blotchy face as we head for the bookstore that is his prize for being such a good boy. "I'm not," I snuffle. Now I had seen Albion, had seen what I had only pictured in my mind for so many years. It was in some ways what I had envisioned. It certainly had the aura of dinginess and low aims that I expected. If you lived here, would you be desperate to get out, desperate enough to deal drugs or engage in prostitution or stealing to get easy money for a ticket to a nicer address? And that new address might end up being San Quentin Prison. Still, even in this bleak place, the balance could shift like a seesaw; it is home to pimps and ex-convicts but also poets like Rod McKuen. Gentrification was happening all over the city, and maybe someday, this street could be home to scientists, professors, and archaeologists and men and women who could walk on the moon.

Sally felt compelled to make friends in low places, to go to these rundown neighborhoods, all in repudiation of her own comfortable life. Everything was tilted in her favor. Why did she insist on turning the opposite way, like Sisyphus struggling to roll a boulder uphill? She wanted to be a savior. If I'd just returned her call the week before her death, could I have saved her? But I never got the message until she was already dead. "OK, let's find you a book and then ice cream!" I smile, and Brendan's grin, with dimples that my kisses get lost in, warms my aching heart.

In January of 1997, the *Chronicle* reported that "Pat Singer, 50, an artist, breast cancer activist and former officer with the United Prisoners Union, died of breast cancer yesterday in her San Francisco home. A native of Cleveland and graduate of Ohio State University, Ms. Singer came to San Francisco in 1972 and began working with the Bay Area's emerging prison reform movement. In 1973, she met and married Wilbert 'Popeye' Jackson, one of the seminal figures in the movement, and served for a time as an officer of the United Prisoners Union, which Jackson co-founded. Mr. Jackson died in 1975, and Ms. Singer later remarried.

"A pioneering breast cancer activist, Ms. Singer was featured in the 1978 film, 'Life After Breast Cancer,' a documentary about the disease . . ."

★ ★ ★

2009

I'm on a gurney wheeling into the operating room. Barb, my pastor, is with me. My husband and kids are left behind in the waiting room, but Barb is allowed in the inner sanctum where only God and clergy and surgeons can go. I've had three months of chemo after a routine mammogram showed I had stage 3 breast cancer in the right breast. I'm bald as an eagle; my hair won't grow back for months. I have neuropathy, which is doctor-speak for *everything hurts*. My feet feel like I have sand in my shoes. I also had to give myself a shot every morning for nine days at the beginning of each chemo cycle. Junkies, how can you stand those needles? It's brutal! At the end of my chemo, I received a Certificate of Achievement "for having successfully completed A Course of Chemotherapy. Congratulations to Lee Darby for having the courage and commitment to persevere." Of course, every canceree gets one of those, same as all eight-year-olds get a trophy in Little League.

When the mammogram nurse showed me my films, I was certain someone had spilled coffee on them. I can't have cancer! I'd been avoiding the mammogram for several years. My HMO had hounded me, e-mailing and calling me at home (which I really should thank them for). I said I had to work and it wasn't *at all* convenient. They countered with "Fine, we have appointments until 8:00 pm." I took the last night appointment and proceeded to subject my breasts to the smooshing from all sides that I was dreading. I secretly suspected that mammograms were the leading cause of breast cancer. The nurse must have seen a preview of my mammogram because I was told to return the very next morning when I got the bad news. I started chemo the day after Christmas—happy holidays! I was working full-time, and a couple of my coworkers "donated" sick leave to me to use when my sick leave got used up.

When the chemo was over with, still, surgery was required. "Why?" I asked. My oncologist said *even* though I had months of chemo to kill the cancer cells, we now need to remove the tumors in the breast and any of the lymph nodes that may be diseased. I opted to remove both breasts, even though my surgeon said my left one was "healthy tissue," to which I replied, "For now." I knew if cancer could attack one breast, it could come back in the other. Thus, I was treated to a twofer, a double mastectomy. All the lymph nodes in my right arm were also removed.

I had an older neighbor who went through the same cancer regimen a few years earlier, but she only wanted to have the affected breast removed and leave the other. I asked her why, and she said, as if it made perfect sense, "I'm in real estate!" And after ten years or so, the cancer did come back in the remaining breast, so she had to go through the whole mastectomy thing again. What a dope. I knew that a number of younger cancer patients had chosen to reconstruct the missing breast by stretching chest tissue over an implant, a process which takes months of what must be a painful and prolonged recuperation. No, thank you! Why would I want to subject myself to months of more pain? I don't even have pierced ears.

Finally, I'm in the recovery area. My husband and kids stand at the bottom of my bed. I didn't want them to come. I want them to see me at my best, not my worst. God, why am I so vain? As if to award their loyalty, I retch into a kidney-shaped plastic bowl, and they avert their eyes. "But you're missing work," I say. "I can take a day off when my mom has had major surgery," says Brendan. So sweet. Liz gives me a funny card with a cartoon of a patient with his butt showing through the open back of the hospital gown. I thank God I am so lucky, so blessed, to have drawn these two out of our gene pool crapshoot. Bruce looks concerned and scared; he's always hated hospitals. I lay there on my back with drains on each side burrowing into my chest. When I get home, I have to empty the drains several times a day; they are attached to my body like nursing kittens. The squeeze bulbs have to be emptied and their amounts recorded. This goes on for many weeks until the liquid diminishes enough, and when finally I see the surgeon for the last follow-up, he rips the drains out of my skin as if they were Velcro. It hurts like hell, but then, everything hurts . . .

I adjust quickly to having no breasts. I always found bras rather uncomfortable. (For years, when I got home from school or work, the bra came off after the shoes.) Once my chest area heals, then I endure radiation treatment five days a week for six weeks. My HMO has a contract with a radiation facility in Rohnert Park, so I drive forty-four miles every day, each way, to get zapped. They created a plastic mold so that my arm can be in the exact same position every day while I lay immobile on the table. They even gave me tattoos, tiny dots to show where the technicians should focus their equipment. The machine doesn't make much more noise than a hum, and it doesn't hurt. It takes all of five minutes.

My drive to Rohnert Park each day is oddly exhilarating. It is a beautiful summer, and I'm on medical leave from my job at the firm that was doing construction work at San Quentin. During the drive, I think I am free! *I am really alive!* I blast The Pogues on my car CD player, and I can't help but feel pure joy. I'm on medical disability, and my days are mine alone. Sometimes I drive back via Sonoma and stop for a snack or a browse in some stores. The final week of the radiation isn't so joyful, however, as I begin to get red and sore. On my second to last day of radiation, a Friday, I complained about the large red welt on my chest. Actually, it was magenta, and it really hurt. Several doctors crowded into the exam room to pass judgment, and I felt like I should invite the rest of the staff, maybe the people in the waiting room, to "Come on down, folks, take a gander!" I said, "Can I just skip the Monday treatment?" In addition to the obvious severe radiation burn of the area, I needed to be back at work or face "mandatory dismissal" according to the terms of my medical leave from my job at San Quentin. The doctor said I should have the final treatment. One of the nurses said, "If the cancer ever comes back, won't you feel stupid for not having it?" So I hauled myself up there, on my lunch hour that Monday, my first day back at work, for one last zap, feeling stupid. I scored another certificate:

Be It Declared to All Present That Lee Darby has completed the prescribed course of radiation therapy with high order of proficiency in the science and art of being cheerful, has demonstrated outstandingly high courage and has been tolerant and determined in all orders given and is thereby entitled to this AWARD OF MERIT

There was even a gold star.

★ ★ ★

Then came 2012's *Season of the Witch* by David Talbot. It is a book that claims to be a "true history" of the 1960s and 1970s in San Francisco. It was described as a national best seller and "a gripping story of San Francisco in the turbulent years between 1967 and 1982."

Author David Talbot writes of Randolph Hearst during the time of his daughter's kidnapping and the People in Need program: "Randy's most surprising new friend was Wilbert 'Popeye' Jackson, the iron-pumping forty-four year old black ex-con who led the radical United Prisoners Union . . . Like Cinque (Donald DeFreeze), whom he had known behind bars, Popeye Jackson also had a reputation as a police snitch. Randy brought Jackson into the PIN operation and treated him like a prized executive. He offered to underwrite a private school education for his ex-con's son. He made sure that Jackson's prison reform work got glowing coverage in the Examiner, and it was no surprise when the paper editorialized that Jackson should remain a free man despite a parole violation for drug selling. Two weeks later, the state parole board agreed. In return, Hearst asked that his new friend tell him anything he heard about the SLA's movements and Patty's whereabouts. They had a gentleman's agreement."

Jackson was flattered by all the attention he was getting from his Hillsborough booster, Talbot said. "'Hearst has great respect for me as a man, and I respect him,' the ex-con told friends. But the unusual relationship did nothing for Jackson's reputation on the street. When his parole was not revoked, some Bay Area militants speculated that he was an informer—not only for Hearst but, worse, also for the FBI."

Then Talbot goes on to describe the murders on Albion Street, "Jackson, accompanied by a woman named Sally Voye, didn't want the party to end. Voye, another one of his white admirers in the United Prisoners Union, and also an undercover narcotics agent, was burying her face in Jackson's lap when a man walked up to the car and emptied the clip of a 9-millimeter automatic pistol into the couple, killing both of them."

According to Talbot's account, it was Sara Jane Moore who had "helped seal Popeye Jackson's fate, circulating a letter among Bay Area radicals that accused him of being an informer for Randy Hearst. Rolling Stone later called it Jackson's 'death warrant.'" Talbot alleges that Sara Jane Moore had been an FBI informant ever since the PIN program had wound down.

A dam broke in me when I read the Talbot account. Once again, I was outraged. How *dare* he impugn my sister like that. I wrote to Talbot in care of Simon and Schuster. I pointed out he had the day wrong (it was June 8). I disputed his statement that Sally was a narcotics agent. She was a kindergarten/first-grade teacher. She had volunteered at a literacy program at San Quentin where her path crossed that of Popeye Jackson. She subsequently became friends with Popeye and his wife, Pat Singer, and joined in their group's efforts to improve prison food, visiting areas, and other conditions where prisons needed improvement. She had seen the shabbiness at San Quentin and agreed that change was needed. But she lived in Benicia and taught school in Vallejo, a good hour's drive from San Francisco, and she would never have had the time or the inclination to work as an undercover agent, period. This is the *fiction* that the Tribal Thumb, a gang of ex-cons and thugs, had put out in a "communique" printed in the *San Francisco Chronicle* a few days after the murders in order to deflect police investigation into their own activities. Talbot bought into the Tribal Thumb lie as if it was the truth, and it had apparently become part of 1970s folklore.

I thought back to what was written in those dozens of newspaper articles after the murders. "She was in the wrong place at the wrong time," "she was an innocent bystander," "she was a witness," and during his trial, her murderer had even said, "She was there, so she had to go." And by the time of her death, she knew where Patty Hearst was. Doncha think if she had been some kind of informant, she would have related that information to police or FBI? Duh. Patty wasn't found for months after the murders.

None of this correlated with some of what was printed long after the murders. "She was a police agent," "she was an undercover narcotics agent," or "she was Popeye's control agent." The story that Tribal Thumb tossed out in order to deflect police investigation didn't work. Richard London, a Tribal Thumb member, was tried and convicted. In addition, two other Tribal Thumb members, Ernest Major Kirkwood and Gary Johnson, were "unindicted coconspirators" in the murders. Was there a deal done behind the scenes? Kirkwood pleaded guilty to two unrelated 1982 murders. Johnson was granted immunity in the London trial. He testified that Tribal Thumb (in the person of its leader, the group's *capo dei capi* Earl Satcher would be my guess) ordered him to kill Popeye Jackson, but he did not carry out the assignment, or so he claimed. Were London, Kirkwood, and Johnson the three-man hit team according to another fellow jailbird who testified at London's trial?

Still, the lie that Sally was any kind of police, narcotics, or FBI informant is still out there, and once something is in print, it becomes some sort of reality unless proven otherwise. It's such horseshit. She was a loyal person, and she believed in the United Prisoners Union. Furthermore, she was *friends* with Popeye's wife, Pat Singer, and wouldn't have betrayed her by any kind of sexual conduct with Popeye.

I called the San Francisco Police Department. Surely, after forty plus years, the truth could be revealed if a person were an informer, especially if that person were dead. A nice police lieutenant told me about the difficulties of identifying informants. "We'd not have many informants if we named names," he said. Dead end there, but I am assured that no civilian (i.e., David Talbot) could have viewed the crime scene photos.

As for the allegation that Sally had her head in Popeye's lap, I don't know how anyone but God or one of the shooters could have observed that at 3:00 a.m. on a dark night. Or was Talbot there, just taking a stroll down Albion Street in the dead of night? How else could this salacious detail be used by an author to titillate his readers? *Unless* he made it up. And if Talbot's book is going be reprinted, he needs to correct the Popeye/Voye murder section to remove those lies. It's what any self-respecting journalist would do. I've written to him to that effect, with no response.

★ ★ ★

I drive down the narrow two-lane street of the town of San Quentin, a village clinging to the steep hillside at the base of the Richmond–San Rafael Bridge. Wild turkeys sometimes come down to the street and peck at their own reflections in the hubcaps of the cars as they line up to enter the prison. I show my badge, and the hinges shriek on the heavy metal gate as the guard lets me into the prison grounds. I drive past the castle turret, the most photogenic part of the entire prison. Make that the *only* photogenic part of the prison. I go past where visitors walk through several gates and get frisked before being admitted in to see their loved ones. I pass the snack bar where occasionally I get some lunch. I skirt around the dull yellow ochre of the East Block and then the road winds past the edge of the individual exercise cages used by the condemned prisoners from the administrative segregation (ad seg), which is prison-speak for solitary confinement. It houses prisoners so dangerous that they cannot even exercise with others. Inside, hidden, is the lethal injection chamber, thought to be more "humane" than the old electric chair. Uh-huh . . . Over seven hundred inmates reside on death row, but no one has been lethally injected since 2006.

San Francisco Bay sparkles off to my left as a Larkspur ferry boat glides by, loaded with passengers heading for their work in San Francisco. The boat's wake fans out behind it in a shampoo froth. A snowy egret, opened wide in flight at my intrusion, is folding himself back up again, settling in on the shore farther down.

I can see now, off to the west, the outline of Mount Tamalpais rising above the delta of the Corte Madera Creek. The Sleeping Lady, the native tribes called the mountain. She lies with one hip turned skyward, the ridges of her hair flowing out toward me, her arm flung out with San Quentin in the palm of her hand. A white plume jet streams across the sky above, as if she is sending signals to Mount Diablo, the devil mountain fifty miles to the east. The thousands of shades of greens and blues seem chosen from a limitless palette to match the weather. I breathe in the tang of the marine breeze as the sun breaks into pieces on the open water.

I then pass the yard where prisoners who are a lower security risk are milling about. I'm back at work from my cancer ordeal, my job filled during my four-month absence by a temp. I park at the quadruple-wide construction trailer where I work for a company that is providing construction management for a $30 million project—we share the trailers with the lead contractor's crew. The project building is a five-story medical, dental, and mental health facility being erected in the heart of the secure part of the prison, if you believe that a prison could have a heart. Several years before, prisoners sued the state, claiming they did not have access to adequate health care. The courts agreed, and this is the first project. San Quentin is the oldest prison in the state, dating back to 1852 when gold rushers who brought lawlessness to the forty-ninth state needed to be separated from law-abiding people. Women prisoners were actually housed here in earlier days. I read that at least one woman was executed here. During the excavation for the new health-care facility in 2009, a basement dungeon from those early days was discovered.

Everyone who works at San Quentin is required to go through an orientation, complete with a written exam at the end. I can still hear the beefy uniformed officer, handcuffs dangling from his belt, saying, "Don't have sex with the inmates," repeating this loudly. The other construction management coworkers and I looked at each other and giggled, as if we would do such a thing. As if we could be influenced by these losers. We were assured by our own employer that for our safety, none of us would have any contact with the prisoners. But the officer continued the mantra, saying it is not uncommon for civilian workers at prisons to somehow become lured into becoming involved with prisoners, feeling sorry for them. "They will try to manipulate you. Don't give them anything. They will laugh at you behind your back," he said. All of us must abide by the dress rules—no jeans, no denim at all, no work shirts, because this is what the inmates must wear. No yellow rain slickers. No smoking. No cell phones.

I have worked here for two and a half years. When I was first assigned to the project, I was concerned that Sally's killer was here, but I found out he had been transferred years before to another prison. I spend my workdays with administrative work pertaining to the construction of the new building—one part of my duties is to gather the names and info of the various workers and tradesmen who come into the prison grounds each day to work on the new health-care building. Each worker must be vetted on a Department of Justice database—felons need not apply; they will not be allowed to enter the prison grounds to work even for a short time. Once a day, I walk (or take an electric golf cart) over to the warden's office and present my list of tradesmen to his assistant. There are only a couple of prison employees authorized to run the names at a computer in a mysterious room in the bowels of the warden's office building. Usually, one of the guards—custody officers—will bring the list back, and I notify the contractors as to which workers are authorized to enter the prison grounds and which ones are banned. From my window in the trailer, I could occasionally see a minimum security inmate work crew—overseen by a custody officer—weed whacking in the windswept open areas of the grounds or along the pocked roads. When the health-care building is finished, our team will be assigned to another project at a school or hospital or another prison.

I remember years ago coming here with a group from my church to protest an execution. The man scheduled for the execution also killed two; they were teenage boys, and he ate their hamburgers after killing them. Despite our objections, the man was executed the next day, the last inmate to be executed at San Quentin as it turned out. I think back to how I felt when the man who killed Sally was captured. I was relieved, but it gave me no satisfaction, no "closure." It made no difference to me if Sally's killer got life in prison or the death penalty. The only outcome that would have made me happy was to have Sally come alive again, to share with me a laugh and some truth, and to continue with our lives. *That* would be justice, but no agency or power can do that. The robed woman who symbolizes justice wears a blindfold and holds up scales. The scales are always empty, and she can't see.

My stand on capital punishment would be consistent with Sally's views, I think. It had been declared unconstitutional three years before her death, and she and the other prison activists probably felt hopeful that public opinion was swinging toward prisoners. But if I had been the one killed, would she be here with a bullhorn, shouting, "Fry the son of a bitch?"

I still think the man who shot my sister is a monster; he knew what he was doing when he pointed his gun. He was not sentenced to die, but he could have been. I believe he who has killed should not know freedom again; that is punishment enough. To never see wildflowers bloom on the mountain or see the fog creep across the Golden Gate, to never hold your baby or watch your child play in a baseball game, to never sit in a sunny cafe with a cappuccino and laugh with friends, that is punishment enough.

I can't help but wonder what Sally would have said about my employment at San Quentin. Would she think the new state-of-the-art health-care building was enough? Or would she continue to press for more? Better food, more childcare, improved visitor areas, a solution to overcrowding at so many prisons in the system . . . I think I know the answer because I know the truth. She wanted to make a difference.

I also know the answer to the question of whether Sally was an informant or not. There would be the kind of informant who was so desperate for money that he or she would sell out their own grandmother just to get paid. Sally had enough money and a job with benefits. Another kind of person would sign on as an informant because by doing so, cooperating with law enforcement, they could avoid or get reduced punishment for a crime. Sally followed the rules, so she wouldn't have been coerced or browbeaten into cooperating against her will. Again, I know the truth. She was never an informer. She would not have betrayed her friends. She just wanted to change what was wrong in her world.

★ ★ ★

The year 2020 was a horrible year. The COVID pandemic required mask wearing not just in cities, like in 1918, but everywhere, a worldwide plague. In the United States, hundreds of thousands have lost their lives, and so many jobs have also been lost and businesses ruined. The West was still reeling and trying to recover from sky-darkening wildfires with the loss of millions of acres of forest land and thousands of homes the year before. Just when I was feeling smug about having avoided the suffering, my own world wobbles on its axis when I find out after a routine colonoscopy that I have colon cancer. No! I've been cancer free since 2009! No way! Actually, it started with my doctor sending me a "stool kit" as a part of my annual checkup. I immediately thought of the hilarious movie *Waiting for Guffman*, which is set in some Midwest town that is "famous for its stools." That home test revealed blood, and then the colonoscopy confirmed there was cancer. I am deep into my faith now, so I am not afraid. It is not exactly the faith that my grandmothers counted on to get them through earthquakes, the Depression, World War II, and old age. It's my own faith. I finally got to live in God's house. With the grace of God and the support of my awesome family, my fantastic church community, and my loving friends, I'm going to fight this.

Mr. Snoid, *get out*. The doctors have work to do! One of my brother's friends jokingly asked if I'd thought about organ donation after I'm dead. I told him yes, and he can have my colon.

Bruce drops me at the front door of the hospital at 5:30 a.m. No family or pastor this time to hold my hand. I wear my mask like all the health-care workers. I've had a CAT scan. I've had a PET scan. I've had a bronchoscopy. Now I have to have the bad part of my colon cut out and then stitched back up. I hum, "Jesus, remember me when I come into your kingdom . . ." *The lights in the operating room are* so *bright*, my last thought as I drift off into the anesthetic dream. I'm in the hospital for four days, and I don't mind having no visitors. I'm able to talk to loved ones and friends on my cell phone. I beg them to not make me laugh; my stitches aren't really painful unless I laugh or cough. At least nobody, except the nurses, can see me at my worst. I try not to look at the haggard face in the bathroom mirror. I'm on a liquid/soft food diet, but no Jell-O in sight. I finally ask for some, and I get a jiggly square of red Jell-O with my last lunch. When all seemed to be functioning normally, I am cleared to go home. Two weeks later, I return to have the metal stitches removed from the four different incisions in my abdomen. No one is admitted to the office without a mask, a temperature check, and a blast of hand sanitizer. My doctor tells me that the other metal stitches, the ones that patch my colon together inside, are made of titanium. High tech. Cancer is found in the lymph nodes Down There.

As if I needed another cancer, the bronchoscopy revealed that my breast cancer was still lurking in lymph nodes in my chest, including one resting on my trachea. Not operable. Not suitable for more radiation. But who knew? There is a drug that conveniently treats *both* colon cancer and breast cancer. I don't have to go to the doctor's office and be attached to an IV like I did over a decade ago. This time, my regimen includes a chemo in pill form, eight per day (It's happy holidays once again!). If I'm still here next Christmas, we will know if it worked. Blood tests every three weeks reveal to the oncologists whatever it is they are trained to see. I see my doctor on my phone. Meanwhile, I celebrate my life as much as possible without hugs from my daughter and son and their families, especially my precious grandkids. Friends keep in touch online via Zoom. This is life, without haircuts, socialization, dinners out, church, or travel.

★ ★ ★

Still, the world abides, and we learn how to live in it. COVID will be conquered. I wonder what Sally would think of how our world has changed, or not changed, since her death in 1975, such as

- the DNA and the ability to identify a person using microscopic skin cells;
- the Internet;
- Trump;
- computers in every home;
- cell phones that can take photos (selfies!);
- social media that keeps people hunched over their phones;
- US involvement in Middle Eastern conflicts;
- the World Trade Center hit in 2001 by airplanes hijacked by terrorists and destroyed and thousands of New Yorkers killed;
- the COVID pandemic of 2020–21 affecting millions worldwide, ordinary life at a standstill and shelter-in-place quarantines, mandatory wearing of masks, and no school;
- gun control (rather, lack thereof);
- racial distrust and tension that continues despite enormous advances in parity across a broad spectrum of society, including a beloved black president;
- legalization of marijuana (Popeye's nineteen years in prison); and
- Spanx (an important cultural advancement).

I zip up the bright orange sweatshirt I bought at the thrift shop yesterday for this march. I am walking across the Golden Gate Bridge with some friends from church, joining a larger group called Mothers Demand Action. We wear orange, we have signs, and we shout, "No more silence! Stop gun violence!" The strong wind carries our words into the fog. Cars rushing past on the bridge honk their horns, and people wave their support out of their open car windows. I'm almost at the place on the bridge walkway where Mom threw the nosegay of white roses and daisies into the slate gray water for Sally forty plus years ago. I wear a big plastic button that says Survivor. Hundreds of us, mostly women but some men and children, walk the bridge in protest of gun violence, as if we could save the innocent schoolchildren, concertgoers, and ordinary workers in too many places around our country who have already died by gunfire. Maybe I can't save them. I couldn't save Sally. But like her, I have to do something.

We have stars in our eyes.

ACKNOWLEDGMENTS

This memoir was conceived long ago at a writing workshop with Anne Lamott. After that I continued to meet regularly with other writers from that workshop: Diane B, Valerie, Diane E, Elizabeth, Kay and Hella. I thank them for their thoughtful encouragement.

I continue to be inspired by the writing of Anne Lamott, Elizabeth Gilbert, Kelly Corrigan, Lionel Shriver, and the late Nora Ephron. I am spiritually sustained by my wonderful faith community, Westminster Presbyterian Church and its pastors, Doug, Barb, Rob and Bethany.

And I am immeasurably grateful to have the love of Bruce and our children Liz and Brendan, and their families. You are my stars.

ABOUT THE AUTHOR

Lee Darby is a writer and amateur quiltmaker who lives in Northern California with her husband.

CPSIA information can be obtained
at www.ICGtesting.com
Printed in the USA
LVHW091227290721
693809LV00012BA/768/J

9 781664 167841